YOU *Have* TO KNOW

ENDORSEMENTS

"Melanie is one of a kind!! Her life story is filled with God's glorious grace & love ... and miracle answers to prayer. Her family is a testament to her devotion to both them and Christ. Vivacious, generous, beautiful inside & out ...I know this book will light up your faith to believe God for your own miracles! I count Melanie as a friend to both myself and our family."

- PS CHRIS PRINGLE
CO-FOUNDER, CHURCH GLOBAL WITH HER HUSBAND, DR PHIL PRINGLE

"This is fantastic! If I could boil it down to one word: relatable. To the point where you are absorbed in the story and how it relates to your own life."

-DOREY BLACK
DIRECTOR, AMERICAN VALUES

"This is what our generation (Millennial / Gen Z) NEEDS to hear. There is so much worth and expectation not only of ourselves but of our parenting and who we are. The value in perspective of this book is priceless."

-CRISTA CRAWFORD
LIFE & CAREER COACH, DIY BOSS & INTERIOR DESIGN CONSULTANT

"Melanie is a rare gem—raw, hilarious, and full of depth. It's been a joy to not only call her a friend but to witness the stunning gift God placed inside her come into full bloom. As someone who's traveled the world, I can say it's rare to find someone who gives so selflessly. Melanie is one of those few. She once told me, "I'm the type of person who had my finger in the electric socket and everything still worked out for good." I laughed—because it's true. Her life is a living Romans 8:28 testimony. This book carries grit, honesty, and Jesus—and I believe it will deeply impact every reader hungry for something real!"

-LINDY-ANN HOPLEY
FOUNDER + REVIVALIST, BEAUTIFUL WITNESS MINISTRIES

FOREWORD BY MATTHIAS WALTHER

YOU *Have* TO KNOW

Melanie Cox

What I've lived.
What He's shown.
What you need to know.

YOU HAVE TO KNOW

www.beautifulwitness.com/publishing |
pr@beautifulwitness.com

Printed in the United States of America.
ISBN: 978-1-968070-02-1 (Paperback)

Cover design: Hannah Cox.

Published by Beautiful Witness Publishing
Beautiful Witness Publishing is a division of
Beautiful Witness Ministries, 501(c)(3)
www.BeautifulWitness.com

Printed in the United States of America.

DEDICATION

To my incredible children, for sharing your stories with me—every lesson, every laugh, even the embarrassing ones—and for your patience and support along the way. Your friendship and love mean the world to me. I adore each one of you!

To my husband, who has had to put up with all my nonsense, my stories—embarrassing and otherwise—and yet, loves me just the same. Your patience, humor, and unwavering support are my foundation. Thank you for always standing by me

And to Jesus, who never fails me, you are truly my best friend. Thank you for guiding me and giving me strength when I needed it most.

This book is a **reflection of the love, grace, and endless patience that surround me every day.**

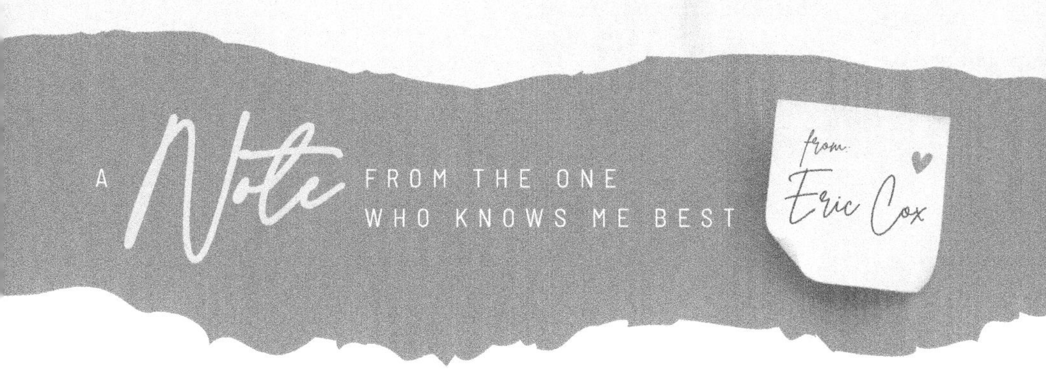

For more than thirty years, I have been blessed to walk through life with my wife—a woman of deep honesty, boundless adventure, and unwavering faith.

She is not only a wonderful wife and mother to our five kids, but also one of the funniest and most genuine people I know. Her love for God and for others shines through in every part of her life, and it is that same light that radiates through the pages of this book.

My wife has lived these words. She has wrestled with them, trusted them, and applied them in the ordinary and extraordinary seasons of life. And now she shares them with you, not as theory, but as a testimony.

It is my honor to commend this work to you, and my greater honor still to commend the woman who wrote it—my wife, my kids supermom, and my best friend for the past three decades.

I hope her words bless you as richly as her life has blessed me.

Eric Cox

ACKNOWLEDGEMENTS

A special thank you to Eric, my ghostwriter and behind-the-scenes hero. Every time I finished a chapter, you would wake up early, make it better, and bring it to life. Who said nerds aren't foxy? Your support, patience, and talent made all the difference.

To my sister Lisa and my kids, thank you for encouraging me to publish what was meant for you alone to know—and convince me that everyone needs to know the love of the Father. Your love and support gave me the courage to share our stories with the world.

And to Lindy-Ann, who not only kept me organized but pushed me beyond my comfort zone because she believes in my voice. Your faith in me has been a powerful gift.

This journey wouldn't be the same without each of you.

Thank you from the bottom of my heart.

TABLE OF *Contents*

FOREWORD

"Melanie is the real deal. She is a force of nature. Inescapable, authentic, curious, entrepreneurial, God-seeking, and incredibly generous. And she is a storyteller with a wealth of experiences. This book is a result of her journey. She doesn't pretend to have it all figured out. Instead, she is generous with her stories and experiences, too. She shares, passes forward, not as a theologian but as a fellow traveler in pursuit of God's purpose for our lives. I hope you will accept her invitation and dive into these life lessons with her. If you do, you will be equipped, inspired, and drawn closer to God, our limitlessly loving Father."

- MATTHIAS WALTHER
CMO, MUSEUM OF THE BIBLE, WASHINGTON DC.

Hi Friend,

Thank you for picking up this book.

My prayer is that as you turn these pages, you'll encounter the goodness, grace, and unfailing love of God in a fresh way.

May His presence draw you closer than ever before and remind you that you are deeply seen, known, and loved.

With love and fierce faith,

Melanie Cox

AUTHOR'S BIO

Melanie Cox

Melanie Cox is a Jesus-loving truth-teller, wife of 30+ years, and proud mom of five miracle kids. She's known for her bold faith, outrageous stories, and ability to bring hope and humor into even the messiest moments.

From parenting meltdowns to personal breakthroughs, Melanie's journey is a living testimony that God meets us right in the middle of our mess—and rewrites the story with love, purpose, and freedom.

She's the author of *You Have to Know*—a raw, real, and refreshingly funny devotional for women who are tired of pretending and ready for honest faith. The book shares 20 powerful stories of healing, identity, and encounters with God's truth.

A successful entrepreneur, Melanie is the founder of Blue Oak Rescue (which saves horses off slaughter trucks), and CEO of multiple companies, including Cox Family Funding, EMC Property Management, and Monarch Real Estate Holdings.

But her greatest joy? Raising five children who know they are deeply loved—and who know Jesus as their Lord and Savior.

Melanie is also a rising voice in women's ministry and has been invited to speak at Bible studies, women's events, and podcasts across the country. She's passionate about helping women know the depth of God's love, break free from the lies of the enemy, and walk confidently in who they were created to be.

Her life motto?

"Thank You God—today is my best day ever."

Preface

Two years ago, I heard a whisper that changed everything. It wasn't a booming voice from the heavens or a dramatic sign etched in the sky; it was a quiet nudge, a gentle prompting from God: **"Read the Bible from the beginning to the end."**

I had been a believer for years, dipping into Scripture like a casual visitor, flipping to the comforting psalms, the bold promises of the New Testament, or whatever chapter God seemed to highlight for me in a given season.

But this was different.

This was an invitation to walk through the entire story, from Genesis to Revelation, with no skipping or shortcuts.

I'd never done it before, and I didn't know what to expect.

At first, it felt like a duty, Genesis with its creation and chaos, Exodus with its miracles and grumbling, Leviticus with its endless laws. I'd always seen God through a lens of awe or curiosity.

How cool that He parted the Red Sea. How harsh that He didn't allow Moses into the Promised Land. I mean, seriously, he just hit a rock; I do worse EVERY DAY!

But as I pressed on, page by page, something shifted.

For the first time, I wasn't just reading stories about God's power or His judgments;

I was seeing His heart.

It unfolded slowly, like a sunrise creeping on the horizon. In the rebellion of Adam and Eve, I saw a Father who didn't abandon His children but clothed them, even in their shame.

In the wilderness wandering, I saw a God who provided manna day after day, longing for these people to trust Him.

Even in the moments that once seemed severe, like Moses gazing at Canaan from a distance, I began to sense a deeper story: A God who loved His servant too much to let him carry the weight of broken people into a land he couldn't fix.

Over and over, I saw it: God's heart, yearning for a relationship with His children, aching as they turned away, rejoicing when they returned.

As I read, my own life started to spill onto the pages. The Israelites' grumbling mirrored my own complaints.

Their golden calf echoed the idols I had built for myself.

Success, comfort, control.

Their longing for Egypt felt like my own pull toward old habits. I couldn't help it; I started to journal. At first, it was just a few thoughts scribbled in the margins of my Bible, but soon it became a flood.

One notebook turned into two, then four, then twelve. Two years later, I sat surrounded by stacks of journals, each one a testament to a journey I hadn't expected.

A realization of the truth of who God was.

One morning, as I flipped through those worn pages, I heard that whisper again: **"They have to know."**

It stopped me cold.

"They have to know how much I love them. They have to know how I'm in every aspect of their life. They have to know that I see them, that My thoughts about them are as numerous as the grains of sand on the ocean floor."

Not just in our lifetime, but He thinks about us that much just in one day.

"They have to know that I'm their Father and their friend, the author of life, and that I love them so, so much."

Tears blurred the ink as I realized this wasn't just about me anymore. *This was a story bigger than my own, a love letter from God to anyone who would listen.*

I think of Psalm 139:17-18: "*How precious to me are your thoughts, O God! How vast is the sum of them! If I were to count them, they are more than the sand; I wake, and I am still with you.*"

With you in all the highs and all the lows.

With you in every moment of every day.

That's what I found in those two years, in every chapter, every verse, every scribbled journal entry: *a God who sees.*
Who knows.
Who loves beyond measure.

And now, I can't keep it to myself.

YOU HAVE TO KNOW IT TOO!!

Chapter 1

The Wild Perfection of Kylie

"The Lord does not look at the things people look at.
People look at outward appearance,
but the Lord looks at the heart."
1 Samuel 16:7

The Bible brims with stories of God finding beauty in the rough-edged, the overlooked, and the gloriously untamed, and none speaks this clearer than David's anointing in 1 Samuel 16.

When Samuel arrived to choose a king from Jesse's sons, the family paraded the eldest—a towering figure, strong-jawed, the kind of man who looked the part. Everyone assumed he'd wear the crown.
But God stopped Samuel cold.

"Do not consider his appearance or his height, for I have rejected him."
Why would God reject the obvious?

To the world, he was everything a king should be.

But the Lord does not look at the things people look at.

People look at the outward appearance, but the Lord *looks at the heart.*

David, the runt of the litter, a shepherd boy with windblown hair and a sling in his hand, was God's anointed. Perfect, not for his stature, but for the fire in his soul, his love for God, his willing heart, his obedience, and his kindness to others.

To God, he was the chosen king, despite what the world thought him to be.

And then there's Gideon: a man threshing wheat in a winepress, hiding from the battle, hiding from the Midianites.

Judges 6:12 tells us that when an angel appeared and declared, "*The Lord is with you, mighty man of valor.*"

Gideon balked.
"*Mighty man of valor?*" he asked.
"*My clan is the weakest in Manasseh, and I am the least in my family.*"

Gideon wasn't feeling it.

He was the Gollum in The Hobbit story, Dobby the Elf in the Harry Potter series. He argued with the angel.

Gideon saw himself through the lens of the world.
He couldn't see himself as God saw him.

But why did he think he was the worst? As the least of men? Dobby the Elf? Who told him that? Was his family perhaps always comparing him to his stronger brothers? Or was it his tribe? His friends? Maybe the Midianites, grinding him down until he believed it himself.

This is what the world will constantly show you—that you are the least, the lowest, unworthy.

It's one of the enemy's greatest tricks. And time and time again, we listen.

Even worse, we agree. We align ourselves with lies.

Yet this isn't how God sees us.

God saw a warrior where Gideon saw a nobody.
God didn't define him by the world's standards.

Through the Father's eyes, Gideon was a *leader* who'd topple altars and free his people.

Gideon was not the least—he was the *greatest.*
Not because of what *he* had done, but because of *who he truly was in God's design.*

All Gideon had to do was cling to that truth, to trust the voice that called him "mighty" when he felt small. And that *trust* led him far.

Through God's eyes: He was never small but a *victor* waiting to rise.

That same truth crashed into my life through my daughter Kylie—a living lesson in seeing ourselves through our Father's eyes. A lesson that unfolded in the most chaotic, unforgettable way. Kylie roared into our world like a storm, a burst of delight we couldn't contain.

We toggled between calling her *Ky-Zilla* and *Ky-Kong,* titles she earned with her wild streak and knack for *destruction.* From the moment she could stumble forward, she was a walking whirlwind—books yanked from shelves, juice flying and splattering across rugs, and curtains dragged down with a giggle.

Her older brothers, Will and Sean, would toil over block towers that grazed the ceiling or cushion forts with hidden nooks, only for Kylie to plow through them like a tiny Godzilla. *"Ky-Kong's back! MOM! GET HER!!!"* Will would holler, half-amused, half-annoyed, as Sean dove to rescue the ruins from her gleeful rampage. She'd survey the wreckage, beaming, deaf to the groans. She'd scale trees and pluck worms off the boys' fishing hooks with a fearless, mischievous grin.

Unapologetic. Vibrant. A force of nature.

My mom, Jackie, didn't see it this way. She watched this chaos with a clenched jaw.
"*That girl needs help,*" she'd snap, her voice edged with concern.
"*She's too wild. Too destructive. She needs a doctor.*"

But my husband, Eric, saw something else. He'd sweep her up, her laughter ringing out, and proclaim,

"She's absolutely perfect, Jackie."

Where Mom saw flaws, Eric saw a gift.

It was the same old divide we see in Scripture. Mom judged the mess of the outward havoc. Eric glimpsed the heart, the way God does. To us, she was *fearfully and wonderfully* made.
Flawless even in the mess.

Thanksgiving Day became her epic showcase.

Outside, the world was shifting to winter, but scraps of fall still clung to the earth like stubborn hope. I sent the kids out to gather what they could: leaves, pinecones, branches, and any flowers still brave enough to bloom.

Kylie took to it like it was her personal art show. In boots and mittens, she marched out into the chilly morning, plucking anything that dared grow—little goldenrod tufts, sprigs of baby's breath somehow still clinging to life, stems of eucalyptus, and one odd crimson zinnia standing alone like it had refused to die just yet.

She made a whole ceremony of it—twirling around with her bouquet, holding each one up to the sky like an offering before tucking it into her basket.

We brought everything inside, and together we made centerpieces—long, lush arrangements that we stretched down the middle of the table like a garland of defiance. We layered in the pinecones, tucked bits of ribbon and cinnamon sticks between the petals, and even placed a few scattered cranberries just for color.

Every detail mattered to me.

Every inch of the table was touched with purpose.

And Kylie—she was radiant.

We got her dressed in her Thanksgiving best: a little tan dress with lace trim and wooden buttons up the back. Her hair was brushed out smooth and tied with a satin ribbon.

She looked like something out of a storybook. Perfect, poised and—if you didn't know her—*angelic.*

But I knew that look in her eye. That sparkle wasn't just joy. It was mischief on the edge of explosion. She was revving up for something.

The house began to fill with the smells of turkey, rosemary, and cloves. The guests arrived one by one, and everyone dressed like they had been plucked from the pages of a holiday magazine—button-downs, sweater dresses, boots polished, hair curled.

It was the kind of gathering that looked perfect in a photo.

But it *felt* like a minefield.

She was five, her eyes glinting with that Ky-Kong mischief, when she claimed her moment. The table was a vision. It was a showcase of the day's hard work—hand-pressed mashed potatoes heaped high, a golden turkey carved to perfection with gravy simmering in its boat, and the legendary table centerpieces—Thanksgiving at its *best.*

Jackie arrived early, casserole in hand and eyebrows already drawn with concern. She hugged me tightly, stepping back to scan the room.

Her gaze fell on Kylie.

"She's still full of energy, huh?" she said lightly, but I could already feel it coming.

"She's excited," I replied.

Smiling tightly.

"Of course," Jackie nodded, placing her dish on the counter. "It's just... she still seems a little, well, *heightened?* You know. Like she's always... *on.*"

Kylie, who'd been spinning in circles, stopped mid-spin and glanced over at Jackie. Just a flicker of a look. But I saw the shift—the look in her eyes.

The line had been drawn.

"She's just *expressive,"* I replied, already on the defensive.

But Jackie kept going, lowering her voice, but edged: "It's not bad, it's just... I don't know. Have you ever thought of maybe having her evaluated again? Sometimes the earlier you catch things—"

From that moment on, with every comment Jackie made about "support" or "tools that might help," Kylie's rebellion intensified.

When Jackie offered to help set the table, Kylie took the linen napkins she'd folded and stuffed them into her sleeves like puppet arms.

When Jackie praised Kylie's artful cranberry sauce swirl, Kylie smeared it across the rim of the platter with a butter knife; one eyebrow raised in challenge.

And the more Jackie said, the more Kylie resisted. She didn't do it with tantrums. No yelling. No screaming. Just quiet, calculated defiance. It was as if she was building a case against every unspoken question, every look that said, *What's wrong with her?*

Jackie never meant to be cruel.

She wasn't mocking. She was concerned.

But concern, when spoken at the wrong pitch, feels like judgment.

And Kylie heard it loud and clear.

By the time we sat down to eat, the air was thick with tension. Everyone was trying to play their part in the picture-perfect holiday. The golden turkey glistening, the rolls warm, and the candles flickering like stars between the handmade bouquets. And then—her moment.

In a flash, Kylie stripped naked, yes - naked. Her clothes in a heaped pile, as she leapt and clambered onto the table. Before we could blink, she was racing its length toward her father at the end of the table.

Bare feet swishing into the potatoes, one wild kick sent the turkey tumbling with a thud, the beautiful simmering gravy dripping into the white carpet, rolls flying into the mouths of eager dogs.

The room erupted—gasps, clinking silverware, outfits drenched in Thanksgiving dinner, and my mom's sharp cry. Jackie's face froze, her lips forming, *"I told you something's not right with that kid."*

But Kylie's eyes were locked on Eric. He threw his arms wide, a grin breaking across his face. She leaped—bold, fearless, soaring—landing safe in his embrace. The dinner, in its entirety, smeared into his linen shirt.

Mom glared, muttering again, *"I told you, Eric, she needs help."*

He turned, Kylie giggling in his arms, and shot back, "See, Jackie? Just what I said—*she's perfect!*"

He grabbed his precious daughter and walked out of the room.

To her dad, she wasn't a mess maker or destroyer of dinner.

She was Ky-Kong.
Unstoppable and perfect, a force of nature designed for greatness.

But to the world?

Well, the world doesn't always see us that way, does it?

It's quick to judge and to slap labels on us like "too loud", "too wild," or "not enough." They put labels on us even when we're only five years old.

It's a mirror that distorts, telling us we'll never measure up. That we're a problem to be fixed. Don't we all feel that sometimes? That the world's eyes are harsh, picking apart our flaws, telling us we're less than we were made to be—the least of the tribe.

Yet her dad's eyes told a different story.
Through them, she was a *hero*, a *conqueror*, a *joy* worth catching mid-flight.

And that's how God sees us, too. Through the Father's eyes, full of love and purpose. God wants good things for us—not because we've earned it, but because we are His.

Don't walk the world looking for evidence that you're not enough because you will always find it. Don't search for proof that you don't belong, because the world will hand it to you.

You're worth and your belonging are not up for negotiation.

Once you agree with what others think, you no longer belong to God.

You belong to their ideal version of you.

If Kylie had let the world define her, she would never have run that table.

But she didn't. She only saw herself through her father's eyes. And that made her unstoppable.

That unwavering belief in herself, rooted in her father's love and pride, propelled her forward with a fierce determination.

She's now in college, finishing her teaching degree, and is almost a pilot. Every bit the force she was when she was little.

Bold. Brilliant. And exactly who God created her to be.

If David or Gideon had listened to the doubters, they would have stayed small and unseen.

The world will never see us as good enough.

It's a broken lens, cracked by sin and shame. But through the Father's eyes, we're more than enough. We're Ky-Kongs, leaping into His arms.

Romans 8:31 says, *"If God is for us, who can be against us?"*

That's the truth we cling to.

God's vision of us is what makes us unstoppable.

So let the world judge.

Let it whisper its lies.

Kylie's dad caught her that day, and God catches us every time we leap in faith.

Through His eyes, we're not just good enough—we're *made* for greatness.

HEART CHECKS, DECLARATIONS & PRAYER

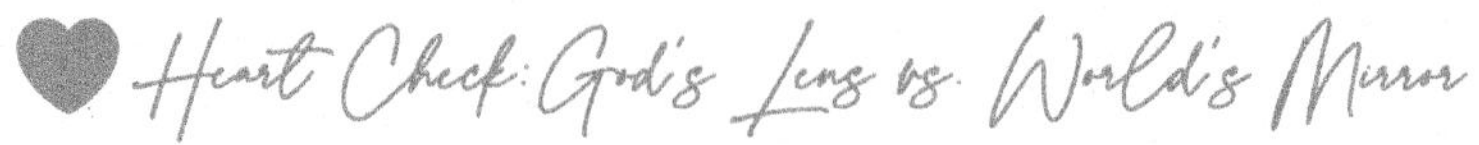

RETHINKING POINT:

Seeing yourself through God's eyes reveals your worth, purpose, and identity as His creation. The world distorts your image with flaws and expectations. Living in His truth means rejecting worldly labels and stepping into divine identity.

QUESTIONS TO ASK YOURSELF:

1. Do I act and conform to what the world thinks about me, or do I live according to how God sees me?
2. Do I believe the world's value system, or God's truth about my value?
3. Do I see myself as fearfully and wonderfully made by God Himself?

REFLECTIONS:

____

____

____

____

____

____

____

____

God is Love

Love
Label

Heart Check: You Through God's Eyes

RETHINKING POINT:

Living from God's perspective frees you to be authentic—not a puppet of passing opinions.

QUESTIONS TO ASK YOURSELF:

1. Am I chasing the world's approval, or rooted in how God sees me?
2. Do I believe the world's lies about who I should be—or God's steady affirmation of who I am?
3. Do my actions align with His truth or the fear of judgment?

REFLECTIONS:

RETHINKING POINT:

The world slaps on labels: "failure," "too much," "not enough." But God sees through love and grace. Choosing His view rewrites your story.

QUESTIONS TO ASK YOURSELF:

1. Do I conform to the world's limiting labels, or align with how God sees me?
2. Do I believe what the world says—or the love God declares over me?
3. What needs to change in my story so God can fully write it?

REFLECTIONS:

BONUS ROUND: WHO DOES GOD SAY YOU ARE?

- Matthew 5:14-16 You are the **light** of the world.
- 1 Peter 2:9 You are **chosen.**
- John 1:12 **Child** of God.
- Galatians 3:26 **Heirs** to the throne.
- John 15:14-15 **Friend.**
- Isiah 44:22 **Redeemed.**
- Isaiah 62:4 **Restored** through the Father's eyes.

DECLARATION TO GOD

God, today I align my heart with Your truth.
I reject every lie the world has spoken over me.
I declare that I am not who the world says I am—
I am who You say I am. I am not too much.
I am not a mistake. I am not forgotten.

I am chosen. I am deeply loved.
I am Your child.
I will not live according to fear, performance, or comparison.
I will walk boldly in my identity as Yours.

Let my life reflect the truth of how You see me.

I belong to You—and that's enough.

PRAYER

Father,

Thank You for seeing me through eyes of love. Thank You for not labeling me by my flaws but calling me by my future. Help me to live from Your truth—not the world's expectations.

Teach me to stay rooted in who You say I am. When I forget, remind me. When I doubt, whisper again. I trust You to catch me when I leap. Amen.

GRATITUDE PROMPT

Write 2–3 things you're grateful for about how God sees you and loves you:

1. ______________________________

   ____

2. ______________________________

   ____

3. ______________________________

   ____

rough faith. And I pray that
u, being rooted and
tablished in love, may have
ower, together with all the
ord's holy people, to grasp

Christ even when we were
dead in transgressions—it is
by grace you have been saved.
And God raised us up with
Christ and seated us with him

And hope does no
shame, because Go
has been poured ou

od is love. Whoever lives in
ve lives in God, and God in
em. This is how love is
ade complete among us so
at we will have confidence

No, in all these things we are
more than conquerors through
him who loved us. For I am
convinced that neither death
nor life, neither angels nor
demons, ... neither the present

be done for you. This
my Father's glory, tha
bear much fruit, sho
yourselves to be my
"As the Father has
so have I loved you

Chapter 2

Black and White Conviction: The Frog Rebellion

"Teach me your way, Lord, that I may rely on your faithfulness; give me an undivided heart, that I may fear your name.
Psalm 86:11

My mom was a black-and-white kind of woman. She didn't mess around in the gray areas of life, and that's what I respected most about her.

She saw right and wrong as clearly as day and night—no blurry edges, no excuses.

She planted her flag on the hill of conviction and dared the world to argue.

It was my junior year in college when I really saw that part of her in me shine like a neon sign. It was the day I planted a flag of *my own.*

I was a psychology major, happily digging into the human mind and psychoanalyzing my roommate's weird habits, when the school hit me with a curveball: a mandatory science lab.

I didn't understand why I had to take it—something about *"broadening perspective."* But there I was, walking into a lab on a Monday morning expecting microscopes and petri dishes.

Instead, I walked into *Frogpocalypse.*

The room smelled like formaldehyde and regret. In the center of it all was a giant box with a couple of hundred frogs hopping around, belting out ribbits like they knew something terrible was coming.

For my frog, it was already too late.

He was unlucky—already pinned down on a tray, still alive but unable to move. Splayed out like a tiny prisoner of war. His little chest rose and fell, his eyes wide open. Those googly eyes locked onto mine, staring like I was Hannibal Lecter.

Mentally, I swear he was telling me about the wife and twenty-three kids he had back home in the pond. Begging for his life.

The professor—clipboard in hand and zero soul—laid out the plan:

"Today we'll slice into its leg. Wednesday, we'll gut the rest."

Then he adjusted his glasses like every Marvel villain ever and added, "Don't worry, he'll be kept alive and comfortable for two days."

Comfortable? Did we have the same definition of that word?

Was I thinking "fluffy blanket," and he was thinking "North Korea"?

That frog looked about as comfy as someone on a medieval torture rack. I wasn't buying it.

This wasn't comfort. This was *torture.*

My stomach churned. My conscience roared. And before I knew it, I channeled my inner Iron Man.

I bolted to the window, yanked out the pins holding the frog's little legs, and shouted dramatically, ***"Go! Live! You're freeeee!"***

I launched him into the air, watching as he flew home to his pond and children...

Except—we were on the second floor.

And he was now paralyzed. He didn't hop away to freedom.

He belly-flopped onto the concrete below with a sad, wet *splat.*

Adrenaline pumping, I knew I couldn't stop there.

I sprinted to the box, ripped off the lid, and unleashed *Frogpocalypse 2.0.* Frogs everywhere.

Bouncing off walls, landing in people's hair. One even did a ninja flip—just to show off. The room erupted in chaos: students shrieking, the professor bellowing, ***"MISS HAMILTON! HALLWAY. NOW!"***

Me? I stood there grinning like a lunatic, knowing I'd just started a *revolution.*

Naturally, I got hauled to the dean's office faster than you can say *"expulsion."*

He sat me down, red-faced and ranting about the cost of frogs. Apparently, they weren't cheap, and now I'd turned all science classes into a disaster.

He dialed my mom on speakerphone, laying out my crimes like he was prosecuting me for frog genocide. I braced myself.

Was I in trouble? Was I responsible for the bill?
Could I get grounded 200 miles away?

The dean smirked as he finished his tirade.

"Anything to add, Mrs. Hamilton? Anything you'd like to say to your daughter?"

Silence. For what seemed like an eternity.

Then my mom's voice cut through, sharp as a blade:

"Yes, I have something to say. Please tell my daughter I'm proud as hell of her. She's living without compromise."

Click.

She hung up.

The dean's jaw dropped.

I nearly fist-pumped the air...
but I controlled myself.

That was my mom—zero gray, all *conviction.*

Every time we did something wrong, my mom used to tell us the same story.

She'd say: "If you toss a frog into a pot of boiling water, it'll jump right out. It knows it's in trouble. But put that same frog in cold water and slowly turn up the heat—one degree at a time—and it won't notice. It'll just sit there until it's frog soup."

Why?

Because its body slowly adjusts to the temperature.

It doesn't even realize it's dying.

Mom never sat still for a slow boil.

She didn't compromise.

She didn't sneak trashy TV or justify content because "we're married."

Didn't swipe a candy bar with a "what does it matter?" attitude.
Never cheated with the excuse of "I earned it."

No white lies. No justifications.

She kept her soul spotless—a five-star Airbnb for the Holy Spirit.

She knew the enemy's game.

If God speaks in a whisper, like He did to Elijah in 1 Kings, then guess what? The devil whispers, too.

He doesn't show up with a pitchfork, screaming, *"Ruin your life!"*

He's sneakier than that. He whispers tiny compromises. One degree at a time. Just enough to warm the water until you're cooked and don't even know it.

If God is in the whisper... Live with conviction.

Or you're just boiling alive, one compromise at a time.

Take Daniel in the lions' den—there's a guy who gets it.
The king made a decree: pray to no one but him.
But Daniel? He wasn't about to bow to that nonsense. He kept praying to God. He lived in conviction even when it earned him a one-way ticket to the lions' den.

He didn't flinch.
He stood firm on God's law.

And what happened?
God shut the lions' mouths.
Daniel walked out without a scratch.

Conviction drew a line in the sand. God honored it.

He was blessed beyond measure because of his conviction.
Proof that conviction pays off—especially when you're on the right side of the Almighty.

He didn't hide behind the curtains or pray silently in his head just to "keep the peace."

Nope.
He flung the windows wide open and prayed the same way he always had.

His conviction wasn't situational—it was constant.

Daniel's not the only one. Flip a few pages earlier and you'll find Shadrach, Meshach, and Abednego staring down a furnace hotter than a July sidewalk in Texas.

The king ordered them to bow down to a golden statue or burn. Their answer?

"Even if He does not [save us], we want you to know...we will not serve your gods or worship the image..." (Daniel 3:18)

That's conviction.
Not because it guarantees safety—but because it refuses to compromise, no matter the outcome.

God ended up walking in the fire with them, and they came out without even smelling like smoke.

Now, conviction doesn't always show up in fiery furnaces or dens full of lions. Sometimes it shows up in classrooms full of frogs.

That day, as the principal sputtered and I smirked, pride surged through me. Sure, my frog liberation project was a messy disaster—RIP, one poor concrete casualty—but I had acted on what I knew was right. Frogs didn't belong in jars; they belonged in freedom.

And my mom? She didn't care about the chaos or the cost.

She saw me standing tall in my own black-and-white moment
—and she saluted me for it.

Here's the truth:

Conviction will always cost you something.

For Daniel, it was a den. For the three Hebrew boys, it was a furnace. For me, it was detention (and a hallway full of amphibians). For you, it might be friends walking away, opportunities drying up, or being misunderstood when you refuse to compromise.

But compromise? That's a *dangerous* game.
Jesus said, "*No one can serve two masters.*" (Matthew 6:24).

Compromise is trying to bow to God and the golden statue at the same time—one knee bent toward heaven, the other bent toward culture. It doesn't work. Eventually, the heat rises.

Compromise is like being the frog in the pot—sitting in warm water while the heat cranks up slowly.

You don't notice until it's too late.

Conviction, though, is leaping out. It's Daniel dropping to his knees when the law said not to. It's three young men standing tall when everyone else bowed low.

It's you refusing to trade obedience for approval.

Compromise today looks sneaky: Staying silent because you don't want to lose approval. Choosing comfort over prayer and obedience.
Justifying little sins because "everyone's doing it".

Splitting loyalty between God and money, God and success, God and popularity.

It's like the frog in the pot—sitting in warm water while the heat cranks up slowly.

You don't notice until it's too late.

So how do we protect ourselves? Stay rooted in the word: "*I have hidden Your word in my heart that I might not sin against You,*" (Psalm 119:11).

Pray for boldness, not escape: The early church prayed, "*Lord, enable Your servants to speak Your word with great boldness*" (Acts 4:29).

Surround yourself with people of conviction: "*Walk with the wise and become wise*" (Proverbs 13:20).

Keep eternity in view: "*Our light and momentary troubles are achieving for us an eternal glory that far outweighs them all*" (2 Corinthians 4:17). Because here's the motivation: Compromise feels easy in the moment—but it always costs more later. Conviction feels costly in the moment—but it always blesses later.

Every "yes" to God is a "no" to slow death in the pot.
Every time you stand firm, you step into the blessing of God's presence and protection.

So don't simmer in compromise.

Stand firm. Leap out. Pray loud.

Live in conviction—or boil slowly.

HEART CHECKS, DECLARATIONS & PRAYER

RETHINKING POINT:

Conviction Over Comfort: When you live for God's truth, comfort is no longer the goal—obedience is. Living boldly may cost comfort, but it leads to deeper peace.

Boldness in Small Moments: Faith isn't proven only in grand gestures. It's in the quiet, uncelebrated moments—when no one's watching and the cost feels personal.

QUESTIONS TO ASK YOURSELF:

1. Am I staying silent or compromising to avoid discomfort?
2. Have I chosen ease over obedience in any area of my life?
3. What would choosing conviction look like today?

REFLECTIONS:

God is Love

RETHINKING POINT:

Trying to please people often pulls us away from our calling. Choosing integrity may not win applause, but it pleases the only One who matters.

QUESTIONS TO ASK YOURSELF:

1. Have I ignored the Holy Spirit's nudge to act on a small but meaningful choice?
2. Do I treat small ethical moments as opportunities to glorify God?
3. Where do I need to be more faithful in private integrity?

REFLECTIONS:

RETHINKING POINT:

Sometimes, standing for what's right doesn't look tidy. Sometimes it looks like flying frogs and a second-floor window. But living with conviction means drawing a line—refusing to compromise even when no one else gets it.

QUESTIONS TO ASK YOURSELF:

1. Do I make decisions based on how others will react, or on what's right before God?
2. Is there a person whose opinion has become louder than God's voice?
3. What would it look like to live today for an audience of One?

REFLECTIONS:

DECLARATION TO GOD

God, I choose to live in bold conviction.
I refuse to be slowly boiled by compromise.
Let my heart burn bright with truth and righteousness.
I will not shrink back to please others. I will stand tall to please You.
I choose clarity over convenience, courage over approval.
I want to be faithful in the small moments—the whispered tests and everyday decisions.
Make me unwavering. Make me whole.

PRAYER

Father, give me the strength to stand when it's easier to blend in. Help me see the places where compromise has crept in quietly. Remind me that conviction matters—not just in the big decisions but in the small, hidden ones. Let my life reflect Your truth. Let my courage inspire others. Let my obedience—even when it costs—glorify You.

Thank You for showing me that living with integrity brings freedom. That it pleases You. That it draws me closer to Your heart. Keep me from the slow boil. Use my life to make waves for Your Kingdom. Amen.

GRATITUDE PROMPT

Write three ways God has honored your conviction, even in small moments:

1. ______________________________
   ____

2. ______________________________
   ____

3. ______________________________
   ____

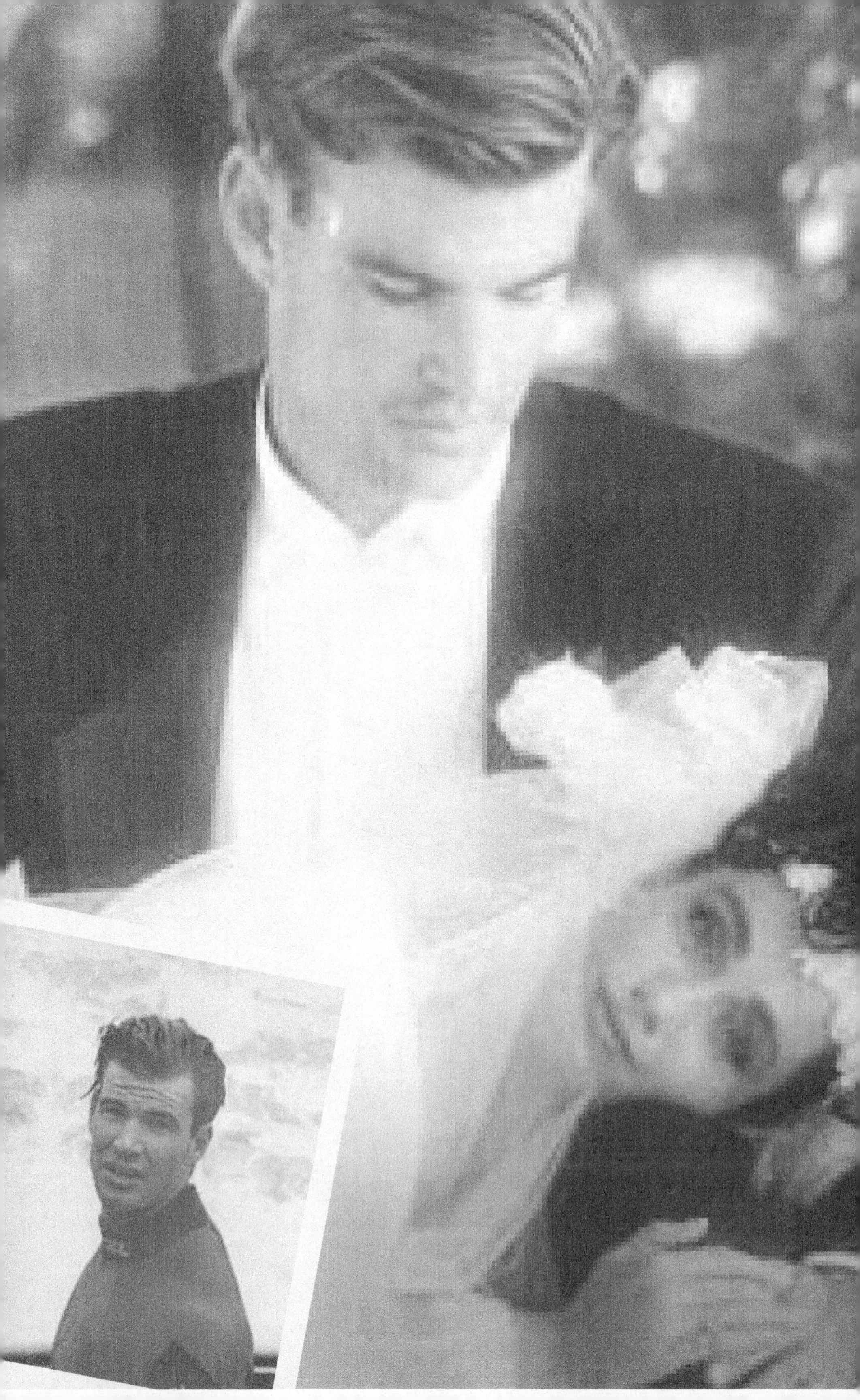

Chapter 3

Trusting God When The Path Isn't Clear

"Trust in the Lord with all your heart
and lean not on your own understanding;
In all your ways submit to Him,
and He will make your paths straight."
Proverbs 3:5-6

Life is full of mystery, isn't it? We crave answers, certainty, and a neatly mapped-out plan.

But here's the truth: **If we demand to understand every single thing God is doing in our lives, we'll miss out on the beauty of His work.**

The goal isn't to figure it all out—it's to trust Him, especially when the fog rolls in and we can't see a step ahead.

God doesn't promise us a detailed itinerary; He promises us His presence. And that's enough.

Let's look at a man from the Bible who learned this the hard way: Joseph. You probably know his story in Genesis. He was the favored son, the one with the colorful coat and the big dreams—literally.

God gave him visions of his family bowing down to him, hinting at a future greatness.

But then, the plot twisted.

His brothers, fueled by jealousy, sold him into slavery. He ended up in Egypt, far from home, working as a servant in Potiphar's house. Later, he was falsely accused and thrown into prison. Years passed—years of confusion, silence, and waiting.

God doesn't promise us a detailed itinerary;
He promises us His presence.
And that's enough.

Can you imagine what Joseph must have felt? **"God, I thought You had a plan for me. I thought You showed me something amazing. Why am I here, in chains, forgotten?"**

If Joseph had demanded to understand every step of God's process, he might have given up. But he didn't. He trusted. He served faithfully wherever he was—whether in Potiphar's house or a prison cell. He trusted God. And then, in a sudden turn of events, God lifted him from the dungeon to the second-highest position in Egypt, where he saved countless lives during a famine—including his own family's.

Genesis 50:20 captures the heart of it all. Joseph, now reunited with his brothers, says, *"You intended to harm me, but God intended it for good to accomplish what is now being done—the saving of many lives."* He didn't understand the "why" during the dark years, but he trusted the "who"—and God turned his pain into purpose.

Here's the thing: God doesn't ask us to understand His ways; He asks us to trust His heart. Proverbs 3:5-6 says, *"Trust in the Lord with all your heart and lean not on your own understanding; in all your ways submit to Him, and He will make your paths straight."* Notice it doesn't say, "Figure it out first." It says to trust and submit—even when the path looks crooked or confusing.

I've lived this myself, and it wasn't easy. In college, I moved to San Francisco, living what I thought was my best life. The city buzzed with energy—parties, friends, late nights. I loved it! In fact, I loved it so much I was flunking out of college (but that's for another book). San Francisco was the place, where I *belonged.*

But deep down inside, I knew I was going astray.

I knew that every late night, every missed assignment, every rave and glow-in-the-dark stick was leading me somewhere I didn't want to end up and making me into someone I probably didn't want to be.

Then one day, my phone rang. It was my sister—the one who never calls just to say hello or chat about the day. It was Lauren, the sister who only calls when she's got something important to say or she's heard a whisper from God she can't shake. It's never a casual "How's your day? I miss you" chat; it's always something deeper.

Her words carry weight, like a storm rolling in, so I brace myself every time her name lights up on my phone. She loves me, I know that, but it's less a warm hug and more a firm grip, like she's been assigned by God to wrangle me back onto the path when I wander too far.

Whether it's a warning, a revelation, or a truth I'd rather dodge, her calls are a tether, pulling me toward something deeper, even when I want to keep things light.

"Hello, Lauren, what's up?"

"Hi, Melanie, God told me it's time to come home," she said.

There it was—not warm and fuzzy or idle chit-chat but a directive from God that I could obey or ignore. Her voice, as always, carried that weight I couldn't ignore. Deep down, I knew she was right. I knew I was a boat drifting without oars, going nowhere, ultimately getting lost at sea.

This was God nudging me through her words, but I didn't want to listen. Leave San Francisco? This amazing place? Why would God pull me away from something I loved so much? Couldn't He just find me a more grounded friend and a church here?

It didn't make sense, but deep down, **I knew it wasn't a light suggestion from God—it was a command, and I had to choose to be obedient or not**. The choice was mine to make.

When I finally said yes, I packed my bags and moved to San Diego, enrolling in the smallest, quietest Christian school I had ever seen, not for some exciting new adventure, but for a place that was a downgrade in every single way.

No raves in San Diego, no secret doors leading to trouble, just the beach, coffee shops, and quiet nights. The oddness crashed over me like a tidal wave as I left the city behind.

I cried for days—big, ugly tears that refused to stay in my eyeballs. The day I moved into my dorm, I sat on the stiff mattress, surrounded by bare cinderblock walls, and sobbed.

My roommate's mom was there, helping her unpack, and she couldn't help but notice. Trying to be kind, she patted my shoulder.

"Oh, honey, you'll adjust, it's just homesickness."

I looked up, red-eyed, and snapped. "I'm not homesick, I'm just unhappy."

She didn't understand, and I wasn't going to tell her. Her face froze—half shock, mostly panic. I could tell she didn't know what to say.

Honestly, having dropped my own children off at this very same college, it must have been nerve-wracking for her and her husband. They would have to wonder if their daughter was about to spend the year with a total lunatic.

I'd sit in that cramped dorm room, staring out at the uninspiring campus, replaying memories of foggy streets and laughter with friends. San Diego wasn't even close to what I'd left.

The college was tiny, the vibe quiet, and the people? Well, they were dorky—awkward, overly earnest.

I had traded clubs for Bible studies. Nothing like the crowd I had run with up north. I hated it. Everything felt wrong—the bland buildings, the slow pace, the way I didn't fit in.

I'd mutter to myself, "God, why here? Why this place? This feels like a punishment, not a plan."

Trusting God in that moment was hard—really hard. I wanted to bolt back to San Francisco, to the life I knew and loved. But I stayed, I obeyed. And obedience to God, I learned, isn't just a checklist—it's an act of faith.

It's saying, **"I don't get it, Lord, and I don't like it, but I trust You're up to something."** You have to live in obedience for God to move, even when every fiber of your being resists. It's like planting a seed in dry soil—you don't see the growth yet, but you trust that God is watering it and the harvest is coming.

Two weeks after I settled into that dorky little college I couldn't stand, I met my *husband.* Just like that, everything shifted. The man I would spend my life with walked into my story because I had said yes to a move I didn't understand.

When I changed my lens, the bland campus by the beach transformed before my eyes—waves crashing from my room, sunlight glinting off the sand, and the quietness wrapped around me like a balm, bringing a peace I hadn't known I needed.

The campus was beautiful! The people I had met at Bible study weren't just faces anymore; they were friends—real and steady, the kind you can lean on, laugh with, and grow alongside.

Looking back, I see it: God wasn't taking something away from me in San Francisco; He was leading me toward something better. I couldn't see it then. Through tears and doubts—I had to trust Him blindly.

Maybe you're in a season like that right now. Maybe you're asking, "God, why this job loss? Why this sickness? Where is my husband? Why the waiting?"

You don't have to understand it all—and honestly, you won't.

God's ways are higher than ours (Isaiah 55:8-9).

But here's the promise: GOD IS GOOD, and He is working for your good. Romans 8:28 says, *"And we know that God causes everything to work together for the good of those who love God and are called according to His purpose for them."*

Your job isn't to decode the plan; it's to hold His hand and keep walking.

Trusting God can feel like a wrestle sometimes—not always easy to master. But when you choose obedience, even when it stings, you're stepping into faith.

Like Joseph, you might not see the palace until you've walked through the prison. Like me, you might not see the blessing until you've gritted your teeth through a move to a place you can't stand.

God's not asking you to understand everything He's doing in your life—because if you did, you'd miss the miracle of trust. And when you trust Him, especially when you don't understand, that's when He'll move in ways you never expected.

God's word says it's a lamp unto our feet—not a floodlight that blasts the whole neighborhood, not a chandelier showing off every corner of the house. Just a lamp. Just enough to see the next step.

And that's exactly how He calls us to walk with Him: one step, one yes, one moment of trust at a time.

It's not only trust—it's obedience.

It's the heart of a child slipping their hand into the Father's and saying, "Lead me, I'll follow."

When we live like that, our life becomes one big "yes" to God. We don't have to know the full map, because the One holding the lamp already knows the way.

And His path—though sometimes winding—is always the one that leads to a life overflowing, the most fulfilled life we could ever dream of.

We are God's cherished children, formed by His hands, and to achieve peace that surpasses understanding, you have to give up the right to understand.

Close your eyes and let Him lead you, trusting He is guiding your every step toward goodness.

And if we can say yes, our lives will be better than we could ever imagine!

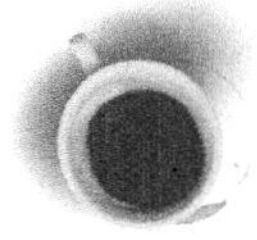

HEART CHECKS, DECLARATIONS & PRAYER

RETHINKING POINT:

When God calls you to step into the unknown, fear of failure, rejection, or uncertainty can hold you back. But choosing faith over fear means believing He's already ahead of you in the journey.

QUESTIONS TO ASK YOURSELF:

1. Are you holding onto something you should be letting go of?
2. Is there somewhere God is leading you, a whisper that you're ignoring?
3. Am I letting fear dictate my decisions, or am I leaning into faith, trusting that God's plan is bigger than my discomfort?

REFLECTIONS:

God is Love

Heart Check: Control vs. Surrender

RETHINKING POINT:

It's natural to want to cling to control when the path feels uncertain or uncomfortable. Yet, following God often requires letting go of our own roadmap and surrendering to His direction, even if it doesn't make sense in the moment.

QUESTIONS TO ASK YOURSELF:

1. Am I trying to force my own way, or am I open to releasing control and letting God lead me where I wouldn't choose to go myself?
2. Can I give God my "Yes" even when I don't like the direction?
3. Do you believe God has—above and beyond what I have asked for—already ordained for me?

REFLECTIONS:

RETHINKING POINT:

Staying comfortable can feel safe, but God often calls us beyond our comfort zones because that's where real growth and trust happen. The unease you feel might be a sign that He's stretching you for a purpose.

QUESTIONS TO ASK YOURSELF:

1. Am I resisting this uncomfortable path because I crave ease, or can I see it as an opportunity to grow deeper in my trust and dependence on God?
2. Can I accept that God doesn't give us detailed plans, and that His presence is enough?
3. Sometimes what feels like punishment is often for our benefit. Can I trust in that?

REFLECTIONS:

____

____

____

____

____

____

____

DECLARATION TO GOD

God, I will stop demanding all the answers.
I will trust You, even when the way forward feels foggy.
You are good, even when I don't understand Your ways.
Your presence is enough. Your guidance is better than my plans.
Lead me, and I will follow.

PRAYER

Lord,
I'm done trying to decode every detail of Your plan. I surrender my need to know and embrace my need to trust. Like Joseph, like Abraham, like the countless faithful before me—
I choose to walk with You even when I don't understand.
Help me hold onto faith when things don't make sense. Help me obey when I'd rather run. Help me trust when my heart wants to fight for control. You've never failed. And You won't start now.
Amen.

GRATITUDE PROMPT

Write three ways God has shown up for you when you chose to trust over understanding:

1. ______________________________
____

2. ______________________________
____

3. ______________________________
____

Chapter 4

Surrender

"For I know the plans I have for you," declares the Lord, "plans to prosper you and not to harm you, plans to give you hope and a future."
Jeremiah 29:11

When I got married, I had a picture in my head of what my life was supposed to look like. I'd dreamed it a thousand times. Standing there in my white dress, my husband Eric smiling beside me, and then a few weeks later, a positive pregnancy test from our honeymoon.

That was the plan.

Kids and lots of them! Running around with sticky hands and loud giggles—and at the center of it all: me as a mom, pouring cereal into bowls, tucking little bodies into bed, living the life I had always wanted.

It felt right, like that was the blueprint that God had drawn up for me.

Doesn't it say in Psalm 127 that children are *a heritage from the Lord?*
A *reward?*

But months ticked by after the wedding, and no baby came. My honeymoon dream faded into doctor visits and disappointments. I started to wonder what I did wrong, as the enemy slowly began to take over my mind.
By the end, I was physically, emotionally, and spiritually *exhausted.*

Almost a year had passed when the job I thought God had me in, a space I had created where I helped abused children, the job that I started out loving, slowly became a reminder of where I wasn't supposed to be.

I prayed every morning on my way to work, asking Him to show me His plan. But He was silent. The days got longer, the work started piling up, and I started to feel like I was *drowning.*

I would come home exhausted, crying into my pillow, wondering where God was. "Are You *not a good God,* with *good things?* ***Are You even God?!"*** Eventually, I snapped. "I'm *done!*"

I quit work one rainy Tuesday, thinking I had failed Him—or maybe He'd failed me. I couldn't tell anymore.
So I stopped. Stopped hoping, stopped believing, stopped moving.
My life at a standstill. Stuck in the grey.

Depression wrapped around me like a cold fog, and I let it live there. I would stare at the ceiling, replaying every doubt in my head. Allowing the enemy to not only plant seeds, but also water them.

"God, didn't you promise me joy and life abundantly?" I would mumble under my breath. "Why is this happening? Don't You see what I want? Did You not promise me *the desires of my heart?"* I typed up and held onto that verse in Psalm 37:4, which now felt like a *broken promise.*

I felt so alone, like He'd turned His back when I needed Him most.

My Bible sat on the nightstand, collecting dust. I stopped picking it up, and eventually I stopped reaching for it altogether. What was the point?

A third year rolled around, and by then, I had given up entirely and put myself to bed. Buried under blankets and resentment, hiding from everyone and everything. Hating my life, my failures, and mostly...
God.

My husband, though, never gave up. One day, he dragged our bed across the room and shoved it right against the window. The sun would flood my face, and he would say, "I love you, and so does God. I'm so thankful I married you. You are enough." I would always argue back. *"Enough?* This isn't enough!" Day after day, he spoke the same thing: "You're enough."

One morning—something *shifted.*

It wasn't big or loud, just a whisper in my heart. I don't even know why, but I grabbed that dusty Bible and yelled to God,

"This is the last time I pick this up. If You have something to say, say it *now!*"

I let it fall open. My eyes landed on Psalm 30:5: "*Weeping may endure for a night, but joy comes in the morning.*" I read it again, slower.

Something cracked in me.

Tears spilled out, not the bitter ones I had cried for months, but softer ones, like rain washing away dirt. I thought maybe the nights have been too long. But what if mornings are coming? What if God hasn't forgotten me? What if it was *time to get up and get out of bed?* I did. Finally.

It started small. I would sit up in bed and read one promise a day. Like Deuteronomy 31:8, "*The Lord Himself goes before you and will be with you; He will never leave you nor forsake you.*" I'd say it out loud, my voice shaky at first, letting it sink in.

I wasn't alone.

He had been there all along, even when I couldn't see it. Day by day, month after month—I stood on God's promises. I am enough, and God loves me. His words became solid ground under my feet. I stopped asking *why* He'd let me fall, and started asking *what* He wanted to do with me *now.*

It didn't matter what I thought my life should look like. What I had drawn up in my head wasn't the point. It was about how God saw my life and, more importantly, trusting that He loved me enough to fulfill me even without children.

Jeremiah 29:11 says His plans are for my *good*, to give me a *hope and a future!* **I had been so busy clutching onto my own ideas for my life that I had missed His masterpiece, His design.**

So I stopped complaining and started doing what I should have been doing all along. I started thanking Him. *"Thank You that I'm the person who would love a child that was not my own."*

Because I thought maybe *that* was a part of His plan. "Thank you for a husband so amazing, so steady, who would pull a bed to a window just to help me see the light."

And in that surrender, something shifted. I stopped demanding and started *trusting.*

I kept thanking Him *every* day for what He was giving me.

Thanked Him for my little house, and the garden that always bore fruit.
I thanked Him for Eric over and over again and even for my fat, lazy dog.

Everything I could think of, I gave thanks.

I had spent so many years begging for the version of my plan.
I missed what He *was* doing.

God was showing me that He *had* me and provided everything I needed. He was teaching me in surrender to trust Him, and in that surrender, He would show up. I mean, *really* show up.

One night, I pulled out a notebook and wrote down every woman in the Bible who couldn't have a baby—Sarah, Rebekah, Hannah, and Elizabeth.

They'd waited, cried, felt empty - just like I had.

But God saw them and opened their wombs, gave them miracles, and turned their mourning into dancing.

I scribbled their names. Their stories. My pen shaking with every word.

Then I wrote at the bottom, messy and bold, *"God, if you did it for them, won't you do it for Melanie?"*

That was my turning point. I started making tea in the morning, sitting by that window, letting the sun warm my face. And I would pray,
"God, thank you for all that I have."

I had reached a place of contentment, resting easy in what God had provided: a simple home, a steady rhythm, a life that felt happy and full, even without children.

Happy and grateful for everything. But still a quiet longing stirred. So I asked God for more, not with a clenched fist or a demanding tone, just a gentle whisper, laying it before Him.

"Lord, if there's more You have, I'd love to see it," I prayed. Trusting His answer, whatever it might be, knowing His plans were good. "I'm standing on Your promises. When You say: *'Joy comes in the morning'* - I believe You!"

And that joy came, like flowers pushing through cracked dirt. Not loud or fast, but steadily.

I was content, content in what God had provided.
God knew my heart and honored my surrender.

And here's what I discovered: When you finally let go, God doesn't leave your hands empty. He fills them in ways you could never expect.

I didn't see it all yet, but I knew His promises were alive, moving, already at work beneath the surface of my surrender.

That year in bed taught me something I didn't expect. *I wasn't in control.*
I thought I was—back when I had my job, my routine, and my plan.

Then, when sadness swallowed me whole.
I saw how small my grip was. I had been holding tightly to my own ideas, and they crumbled.

This is the lesson God taught me.

"Surrender, Melanie. My plans are better."

Proverbs 3:5-6, "*Trust in the Lord with all your heart and lean not on your own understanding. In all your ways submit to Him, and He will make your path straight.*"

I spent so long trying to figure out why I lost my way. Why did God feel so far? But that verse said: Stop! *Stop* with your own understanding, *stop* trying to understand, and *stop* walking your own path.

Just close your eyes and reach your hand out, knowing that He will reach you exactly where you are. Give it to Him. It's ok to not understand, but you have to *surrender.*

"I'm Yours, God. Take my life. Your ways are better!"

God's plans are higher, bigger, wilder, holier. The enemy tried to trap me in the wilderness, but God used even that season—not to break me, but to build me.

Deuteronomy 8:2 says to *remember how the Lord your God led you all the way through the wilderness. To humble you, and to test you—to know what is in your heart.*

That year of depression—it became my wilderness. God didn't cause it, but He met me in it. He used it to strip me of my need to control and to prove that with Him, all things are possible. To show me the power of a promise-making, promise-keeping God. To show me that I am loved.

Did it *hurt?* Of course, it hurt, but it *shaped* me. My character grew roots, patience, trust, and grit. I learned that He's faithful when I can't see a way out. **Surrendering didn't just *save* me; It *grew* my faith into something unstoppable.**

Psalm 30:5 says, "*Joy comes in the morning.*" He "*turns mourning into dancing.*" He leads us through deserts to show us our strength.

My faith no longer waivers. I've seen Him carrying me when I couldn't walk, lifting me when I couldn't stand.

Surrendering your life to God isn't giving up—it's the action of stepping into something *greater.*

Surrendering to God is the *key* that unlocks movement in our lives.

It's a full, no looking back release of control. He can't shape our lives if we keep clinging to our own plans. Laying them at His feet only to snatch them back when doubt creeps in.

It's like dropping a burden and then hovering nearby, ready to pick it up again. We have to trust Him and walk forward, letting Him do the work only He can do.

It isn't just a nice idea- it's a doorway to a purpose bigger than you can dream up. We all have plans, little sketches in our minds of what we think is good. Maybe a steady job, a happy family, or a home full of kids.

But here's the truth: What you have in your head, no matter how bright it shines, is only half as good as what God's holding for you. His vision isn't limited by your imagination: It's wilder, deeper, and perfectly fitted to who He made you to be. All it takes is letting go- handing over the reins and trusting Him to steer.

Think about Peter, the fisherman in Luke 5. He'd spend all night casting nets, hauling up nothing but exhaustion. His plan was simple: Call it quits, clean up, and go home. Then Jesus steps in, telling him to push out deeper and try again. Peter could've stuck to his own script; after all, he knew fishing.

But he surrendered, saying, *"Master, we've worked hard all night and haven't caught anything. But because you say so, I will let down my nets,"* Luke 5:5. What happened?

A haul so massive it nearly sank the boat. Peter's best idea was a quiet morning; God's was a *miracle that changed his life.*

That's what surrender does: It swaps your half-good idea for His overflowing great. The catch is: You can't keep one foot in your plans and one in His. You've got to give it all. Your hopes, your worries, your "this is how it should be."

And not creep back to grab it when you get antsy. Whatever you're picturing, God's whispering, **"I've got more."**

Maybe you see yourself teaching a handful of kids, but He's got a whole community in mind.

Maybe you want a safe path, but He's crafted a bold one that will light up the earth.

Surrendering isn't losing; it's trading up.

So take that picture in your mind, lay it down, and say, "God, You take it from here."

He'll hand you something twice as good, because He's been waiting to all along.

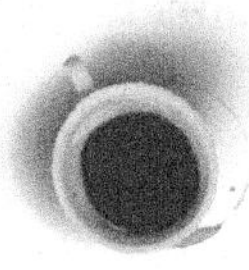

HEART CHECKS, DECLARATIONS & PRAYER

RETHINKING POINT:

Surrender isn't about feeling ready. It's about choosing trust over comfort, even when every part of you wants to hold on. God's plans often stretch us beyond what's easy, but that's where faith grows.

QUESTIONS TO ASK YOURSELF:

1. Am I resisting because I'm scared or stubborn?
2. What's the one thing I'm gripping too tightly? My plans, pride, my fears?
3. Can I take a deep breath and say, "God, I don't want to, but I'll let You have this anyway"?

REFLECTIONS:

God is Love

RETHINKING POINT:

God never failed to show up in the past, and the Bible's proof is your anchor. His faithfulness then is a promise for now—your story is still unfolding, and He's already in it.

QUESTIONS TO ASK YOURSELF:

1. Have I looked at how God came through, like parting the Red Sea or raising Lazarus?
2. Am I doubting He'll show up for me because I can't see it yet?
3. Can I name one time He's already been there for me and let that build my hope?

REFLECTIONS:

DECLARATION TO GOD

God, I surrender every plan I've held too tightly. I trust You with the things I don't understand. You are not late. You are not distant. You are here. Your promises are true. You turn mourning into dancing. You turn waiting into wonder. I give You my whole heart. My hopes. My fears. My future. Because You are good, and You are faithful.

PRAYER

Father,
Thank You for never leaving me, even when I stopped looking for You.
Thank You for whispering truth when all I could hear was fear.
Help me surrender fully—not with gritted teeth but open hands. Show me how to trust again. Let Your word become the ground I stand on. You are the God of Sarah, Hannah, and me. You keep Your promises. Thank You for what You've already done. Thank You for what You will do. Amen.

GRATITUDE PROMPT

Write three things God has given you in this season that reflect His faithfulness:

1. ______________________________
____

2. ______________________________
____

3. ______________________________
____

The Miracle of Will

"Is anything too hard for the Lord?"
Genesis 18:14

The Bible is a treasure trove of God's power over the impossible, and Sarah's story in Genesis 18 has always anchored my heart. At ninety, her body was a monument to lost hope, her womb barren for decades.

When God promised Abraham a son through her, Sarah laughed—not in joy, but in the weary disbelief of a woman whose dreams had faded.

Time, biology, and her own flesh ridiculed the idea. Yet God, unshaken, asked through His messenger, *"Is anything too hard for the Lord?"* Genesis 18:14.

Sarah's laughter turned to wonder when Isaac was finally born, a living testament that **God's promises outlast every human limit.**

That story wasn't just history—it became my foundation.

My own life began to mirror hers in ways I never expected.

For years, I bore the weight of a devastating prognosis.
"You'll never carry a baby!" the doctors declared, their voices firm with certainty. My womb, they explained, was a place where life couldn't

take root—a barren wasteland. My doctor at the time laid it out plainly: "Your womb will never sustain life; it's hostile." **It was a quiet, invisible barrier, but it felt as solid as a wall.**

They handed me adoption forms and surrogacy options as if my story had no other chapters. I'd sit in those sterile rooms, Eric's hand in mine, tears stinging as they shut the door on my hopes.

I'd placed every broken dream at His feet, clinging to His promise: *"For I know the plans I have for you,"* He declares in Jeremiah 29:11, *"...plans to prosper you and not to harm you, plans to give you hope and a future."*

That was my promise, and I held it close.

Then, a woman I'd never met approached me, her eyes wide with conviction, and asked if I was Lisa's sister. Before I could even respond, she declared she'd had a vision:

A *"baby boy"* in my womb, *"a gift from God"*, an *"answer to prayers"*, I'd whispered so many times in *desperation.* I stared at Jeannie, this bold, Bible-fearing woman who seemed to radiate certainty, and something snapped in me.

"F YOU!" I spat, followed by a *long* torrent of words too raw to repeat, with a flood of anger and disbelief I couldn't hold back.

I'd surrendered my life to God, laid down my doubts, and found a fragile peace, yet here she was, stirring it all up again. Even as I cursed her, I knew she'd struck a nerve.

Why was it so hard to believe God could work a miracle for *me?*

Isn't that what faith is supposed to be? ***Trusting in the impossible?***

Clinging to hope when everything says it's absurd? Her words, uninvited as they were, dangling a promise I both longed for and feared.

Leaving me wrestling with the messy truth that miracles feel too big

and too good for someone like me. After my triad, I wasn't thinking about babies. I wasn't thinking about miracles. Honestly, I was still thinking "f-you" in my head: disappointment, grief, anger.
I was raw. And tired. And done.

But then... There was this nudge.
A quiet whisper. Not audible, but unmistakable. *Take a test.*

I laughed. Out loud. "Why would I do that?" I said to no one.

My mind pushed it away—pointless. There's no way.

But my spirit... my spirit leaned in.
I found myself stopping at the CVS.
And grabbed a handful of tests.

I found myself holding it like it meant nothing—and everything.
I took the test. And then, time stood still.

There it was. A pink line. Faint, but firm.

A whisper of life... where there should have been none.

I stared at it. Frozen. Unbelieving.

Tears spilled before I even knew what I was feeling.

Another test.
Then another.
All of them confirmed it.
Pregnant.

Alone in my bathroom, I fell to my knees.
Not in fear. Not in confusion. *In awe.*

I lifted my hands and wept. Not because I was afraid.

But because I *knew.*

The God who parts seas.
The God who raises the dead (John 11:43–44).
The God of impossible things...
He had just walked into my story.

I knew without a doubt:
God is still the God of miracles.

And the one undeniable truth that echoed through my soul was this:

God loves *Melanie.*

Even when the doctor couldn't believe it—
Even when science said no, God had already said yes.

"Your womb—it doesn't make the hormones for this", the Doc said, shocked. He called the other doctors for a second and third opinion. Their faces, filled with confusion and disbelief, hovered over the screen.

I had been in that office many times before, always receiving bad news. Against their expectations, there it was—a tiny heartbeat.

"It won't hold," one predicted.

They couldn't fathom it; they couldn't align this life with their diagnosis of my deficient womb. But I smiled through their skepticism. I knew this was no fluke—it was a *miracle*, a *gift from God.*

God had reached into the impossible and knit life where none should have been.

Because I knew He had given me this, their words lost all weight.

I had faith I hadn't had before—faith that the God who lived 2,000 years ago, the one who walked on water and rose from the grave, was the same God I served *today.*

I knew how powerful my God was, and that truth silenced every doubter.

I'd seen it countless times in my life—
If you have the faith of a mustard seed, you can tell a mountain to move, and it will.

Jesus promised it in Matthew 17:20, and I'd witnessed it—prayers answered, obstacles shifted, miracles born when I dared to trust.

This pregnancy was my mountain, and I spoke to it with that small seed of faith, believing God could move what no one else could.

The journey was grueling. At ten weeks, bleeding sent me straight to the ER, my heart pounding as I braced for what came next. "I'm sorry, it looks like you're having a miscarriage," they warned.

But the ultrasound showed a heartbeat—stubborn and strong.

Nausea crushed me for weeks, my body a storm of weakness.

At twelve weeks, a specialist spelled it out: "Your womb can't sustain this baby."

He urged me to prepare for loss, but I leaned on Psalm 139:13, "*For You created my inmost being; You knit me together in my mother's womb.*" I believed God was knitting this child, stitch by stitch, despite the odds.

I prayed through every scare, every doctor's warning. My hands pressed to my belly, whispering, "Lord, You started this, You'll finish it, because God loves Melanie."

At twenty weeks, the stakes climbed higher. An ultrasound revealed a tear in my placenta, adding another risk. "Bed rest," my Doctor ordered, his tone leaving no room for argument. "Strict bed rest, or you'll lose this baby."

But I couldn't stay still. I had surrendered to God, not to despair. I trusted Him to carry us through. I'd get up to pray, pace the living room with my Bible open, reciting, "*My grace is sufficient for you, for My power is made perfect in weakness*", 2 Corinthians 12:9.

I sang songs until my voice cracked, believing His strength would hold me when my body couldn't.

The hardest fight came at the end. At forty-one weeks, the doctors decided to induce labor, citing my fragile condition and the baby's erratic heart rate, *and* the fact that he was now somewhere between a baby horse and a hippo.

Induction was scheduled for forty-two weeks. I walked into the hospital, a new nightgown folded in my bag, buzzing with excitement about my baby's arrival.

They induced me, and everything *unraveled.*

As the medication hit, my body convulsed—an allergic reaction I had never seen coming. My skin burned, my throat tightened, and the monitors screamed in protest.

My systems started shutting down one by one. My birth canal clamped tight, but I wasn't dilated yet, and he got stuck.

The machines blared as they were recalibrated, what was most women's peak because my resting rate, and I was squeezing him, literally crushing the life out of him.

"The baby's heart rate is crashing," a nurse yelled. "We have to do a C-section!" But it was too late—Will was in the birth canal, stuck and getting crushed to death. Hours of agonizing contractions brought on by the induction ended with his heartbeat fading.

Those erratic, hopeful beeps faded into a single, unyielding flatline, his heart rate disappearing. "We've lost him."

The room erupted in chaos, doctors barking orders, machines beeping wildly. Eric hovered over me. He was a former medic who'd delivered babies before. His eyes met mine, steady but grave, and he said, "This is bad, Melanie... really bad. But no matter what happens, I want you to know how proud I am of you, and I love you. You carried a son, and now we can meet him in heaven. You did what no one thought was possible. I love you. God loves you." Reminding me that nothing else mattered. "You are enough," he whispered.

Everyone thought Will was dead.

I closed my eyes and prayed, "Lord, You've brought us this far. I trust You."

Faith is the substance of things hoped for, the evidence of things not seen. I believed God was bigger than their panic, bigger than their predictions, bigger than death itself. Then—silence stretched into eternity. The room held its breath.

Suddenly, a cry—sharp and defiant—sliced through the tension.

Will, my son, a promise from God, was *alive.*

Ten fingers, ten toes, eyes blinking against the light, lungs roaring to life. A loud pronouncement that: God loves Melanie!

The doctors stood dumbfounded, their mouths agape. "He's perfect," one murmured, almost to himself. "I don't understand," another said.

They called it a tragedy averted by chance, but we knew better.
This was no chance. This was faith. This was God's love manifested from heaven to earth.

When they handed me my son, tears streamed down my face. I cradled him—my miracle, my *promise fulfilled.* I remembered the words the woman had spoken over me months ago, "You're pregnant, and it's a gift from God. He's done a miracle for you."

And now, holding Will, I knew she had spoken the truth.

The doctors couldn't believe I'd conceived, they couldn't fathom I'd carried him, and they couldn't explain his survival.
But I could.

Because of who my God is, Will came out *perfect.*

We just need to stand, to believe, to have faith in His promises. Like Sarah, I'd faced a barren wasteland, and like Sarah, I'd seen God *move.*

Will's every breath is a *hallelujah*, a reminder that nothing—*nothing*—is too hard for the Lord.

Our God is a promise-making, promise-keeping God, but we need to be a promise-*believing* people.

My miracle was realized because I had *unwavering faith*, and I can't express how important this concept is. Our faith must stand resolute, an unshakable anchor amidst the shifting tides of worldly opinion.

The world often whispers, or shouts, that what we see, touch, and measure is truth. The world urges us to conform to its narrow lens of reality.

Yet, we are called to trust in a truth beyond the natural, where the supernatural reigns supreme.

The natural may falter, its patterns and promises bending under scrutiny, but **the supernatural holds fast, defying logic and expectation.**

To waver is to let the world's fleeting noise drown out the eternal whisper of divine certainty. Instead, we must cling to faith, knowing what is unseen often carries the deepest power.

The Bible teaches us this truth in countless stories.
Like the story of David. David tended his sheep, a boy with calloused hands and a heart full of dreams. One day, the prophet Samuel anointed him with oil, declaring him God's chosen King (1 Samuel 16:13).

The Spirit of the Lord filled him, and a promise took root. David would rule Israel. He wasn't a warrior like his brothers, just a shepherd with a sling, but God saw his potential and tuned his life to a divine frequency, a steady hum of purpose.

That frequency rang clear when David faced Goliath. Armed with faith and five stones, he shouted,

"You come against me with sword and spear, but I come against you in the name of the Lord Almighty!" (1 Samuel 17:45).

He slung, the giant fell, and the victory echoed like a psalm. In that moment, David's faith was a pure, unwavering note, and God heard it loud and clear, answering with triumph.

When we live in true faith, it's like a signal, a vibration God attunes to.

John 15:7 says, "*If you remain in Me and My words remain in you, ask whatever you wish, and it will be done for you.*" David's trust aligned with God's will, and the promise felt near.

But the next day, hiding in a cave from Saul's pursuit, David's pitch faltered.

"*How long, O Lord? Will you forget me forever?*"

He cried, words that bled into Psalm 13:1. One moment, he'd praised God's power, the next, he doubted the throne that would be his.

That wavering scrambled the frequency, James 1:6-7 warns, "*But when you ask, you must believe and not doubt, because the one who doubts is like a wave on the sea, blown and tossed by the wind. That person should not expect to receive anything from the Lord.*"

A double mind muddies the signal, and David's prayers hit static.

God's promise didn't fail, but David's lack of constant faith kept him from walking in it.

Twice he held Saul's life in his grasp, once cutting his robe, once sparing him by a spear, and each time faith flickered back, steadying the note.

Yet it dimmed again when he fled to the Philistines, feigning madness to survive. The shepherd who'd toppled a giant lost the rhythm of trust, and the throne stayed distant.

A lack of true, constant faith doesn't cancel God's promises; it muffles our connection to them. David's doubt stretched his journey. From anointing to kingship, David waited, served Saul, running from him. Reigning over Judah at 30, then all Israel at 37. Nearly fifteen years passed because his faith wavered.

When it steadied, the frequency cleared, God heard, and the praise landed. Hebrews 11:6 declares: "***Without faith it is impossible to please God,*** *because anyone who comes to Him must believe that He exists and that He rewards those who earnestly seek Him.*"

True faith is a *constant* signal, not a *broken* broadcast.
David learned this truth.

When we live in true faith, we tune our hearts to God's wavelength. It's not just believing for a moment; it's holding the note steady and sure.

David's story, as well as mine with Will, shows a constant frequency of faith ringing in the heavens. Our song must be sung at full volume, strong and loud, full of faith, knowing God is who He says He is. Unwavering at volume 10.

God hears, answers, and brings the promise home. Doubt delays us, but faith aligns us. When we trust without waver, we don't just wait for God's will; we resonate with it, and He moves. In the cry of a king or of a baby, God shows up. Why? Because God *loves* Melanie.

But, I have a secret that you have to know... *God loves you, too!*

"Let the beloved of the Lord rest secure in Him, for He shields him all day long, and the one the Lord loves rests between His shoulders", Deuteronomy 33:12.

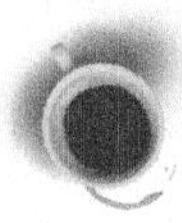

HEART CHECKS, DECLARATIONS & PRAYER

RETHINKING POINT:

A mustard seed of faith, tiny but real, can move mountains when rooted in God's word, not the world's loud skepticism. Even when the odds seem impossible, pushing into the small trust keeps you anchored, knowing God will show up as promised.

QUESTIONS TO ASK YOURSELF:

1. Am I letting the world's doubts smother my small faith, or am I pushing forward?
2. Am I trusting God's word to carry me through?
3. Am I believing the world's report about my odds, or am I clinging to God's word with mustard-seed faith, expecting Him to show up inches away?

REFLECTIONS:

God is Love

RETHINKING POINT:

When the stakes are big, fear can paralyze you, but a mustard seed of faith pushes you to trust God's word anyway. It's not about the size of your belief, it's about standing on it, knowing He'll meet you there and showing up bigger than the world's threats.

QUESTIONS TO ASK YOURSELF:

1. Am I freezing in fear because the odds feel stacked against me, or am I pressing into faith, even a tiny bit, trusting God will show up as I follow His word?
2. What would I do right now if I truly believed God was fighting for me?
3. Am I focusing more on the problem or on the One who promised to never leave me in it?

REFLECTIONS:

____

____

____

____

____

____

____

DECLARATION TO GOD

God,
I don't understand everything in front of me,
but I trust the One who walks beside me.
Your promises don't expire.
Your love doesn't run dry.
Your power hasn't changed.
Even when the world says it's over,
I believe You still make a way.

I choose to trust Your word more than my fears.
To listen for Your whisper above the noise.
To hold onto hope even when it's quiet.

You are my steady ground.
You are faithful.
You are for me.
And I believe—You're not done yet.

PRAYER

Father, here I am again. Honest. Hopeful. Holding onto faith—some days by a thread.

You know every detail, every disappointment, every fear.
But You've also shown me who You are: Faithful. Constant. Powerful. Near.

I don't have to have it all together to come to You.
I just need to come.

So I lay it all down again—every unanswered prayer, every anxious thought.
I trust that You are working even when I can't see it.
Even when it feels like nothing is changing.
Even when I feel small, tired, or unsure.
God, You brought me this far.
You don't quit halfway through.
So I trust You.
I believe You're not done.
In Jesus' name,
Amen.

What I'm Thanking God For Today

Take a moment to pause and remember. Gratitude unlocks peace and refocuses the heart.

1. ______________________________
____

2. ______________________________
____

3. ______________________________
____

4. ______________________________
____

5. ______________________________
____

through faith. And I pray that
you, being rooted and
established in love, may have
power, together with all the
Lord's holy people, to grasp
how wide and long and high
and deep is the love of Christ,
and to know this love that
surpasses knowledge—that
you may be filled to the

Christ even when we were
dead in transgressions—it is
by grace you have been saved.
And God raised us up with
Christ and seated us with him
in the heavenly realms in
Christ Jesus, in order that in
the coming ages he might
show the incomparable riches
of his grace, expressed in his

And hope does not put us
shame, because God's love
has been poured out into
hearts through the Holy S
who has been given to
You see, at just the right
time, when we were still
powerless, Christ died for

THREE TREES

on the day of judgment: In
this world we are like Jesus.
There is no fear in love. But
perfect love drives out fear,

nor the future, nor any powers,
neither height nor depth, nor
anything else in all creation,
will be able to separate us

so have I loved you. Now
remain in my love. If you
keep my commands, you
remain in my love, just as
have kept my Father's

Taming the Wild Horse: Mastering the Battle Within

"Everyone should be quick to listen,
slow to speak and slow to become angry,
because human anger does not produce
the righteousness that God desires."
James 1:19-20

There's a war raging inside all of us—a battle fiercer than any storm, quieter than a whisper, but powerful enough to shape our lives. It's the fight between our emotions and our better judgment, between what we feel and what we know.

Some days, it's like a racehorse without a jockey, bucking and kicking, going wherever it pleases.

And the enemy? **He loves to stir the chaos**, to let our feelings run rampant, because he knows that's when we are most vulnerable.

Emotions are the greatest weapon he can wield against us—they're a gift that makes us human, alive, and connected. But without regulation, they can lead us straight into a ditch.

The Bible knows this struggle well. Look at Moses in Numbers 20. The Israelites are grumbling about water again, and God instructs Moses to speak to a rock to bring forth water.

But Moses is done—fed up with their complaints, his patience worn thin. Instead of speaking, he lets his anger loose, striking the rock twice with his staff and barking at the people.

Water flows, but God said in Numbers 20:12 that *"Because you didn't trust Me... you won't enter the Promised Land."*

Moses' emotions—raw and real—overrode God's instruction, and it cost him *everything.*

This wasn't just about disobedience—it revealed how human emotion can misrepresent the nature of God.

God is patient, merciful, and faithful, even when His people are rebellious.

But Moses, in anger, showed a version of God that wasn't true. It's a sobering reminder that when we walk closely with God, we are also called to reflect Him accurately.

Our emotions are real, but they must be surrendered—because when we act from the flesh, we risk *distorting* the character of the One we *represent.*

Let our response be rooted in trust, not reaction, so that others see God's heart through us.

Sometimes, though, life feels like a playground powder keg—ready to explode with noise, nerves, and pressure.

It was one of those flawless spring days—bright sun overhead, a soft breeze, the school playground buzzing with the chaotic symphony of kids at recess.

It was a Wednesday—the day all the moms were invited to play with their kids.

On this recess, like all the Wednesdays that came before, my son Will sat on the sidelines dreaming of playing kickball. What stopped him? He was too nervous and didn't know where to start.

"What if I get out?"
"What if I mess up?" he said quietly.

I smiled and said, "It's okay if you do. Just have fun—I'll stand here and cheer for you!"

After an eternity of gentle coaxing and epic negotiations, I finally talked my little guy into stepping up to the kickball plate. His tiny sneakers planted like a reluctant superhero, facing his first villain.

I told Will, "No one cares about strikes or getting on the base! It's not the scoreboard that counts, but the sheer joy of kicking the red ball into the wild blue yonder. Making friends and just enjoying recess."

And me, his Mom, cheering from the sidelines, just as I promised.
No helicopter hovering.

The picture of a well put-together, calm, quiet Mom.

Just like every other well-dressed, respectable St. John's Mom, sitting quietly on the sidelines. (Well, it's how I *wish* this story went!)

On this Wednesday, the game was already underway—a whirlwind of red rubber and wild kicks. Kids cheered and groaned with every play, their voices a constant hum.

Will finally got his turn at the plate, stepping up with a look that was half grit, half terror. He looked over, and I gave him a small smile and a big thumbs up.

The pitcher rolled the ball fast. Will swung his leg, connecting with a solid thwack. The ball didn't soar, but it skittered past the infield, giving him a shot. He bolted for first base, arms pumping, and slid in just as the baseman scooped up the ball.

"Safe," I muttered under my breath, clenching my quiet triumph. From where I stood, it was clear as day—his foot hit the base a split second before the tag.

"Out!" a voice barked, sharp and decisive.

I whipped my head around, and there was Julie, standing near the first baseline where her son was playing. Arms crossed as if she owned the place. She was another mom, one of those types who volunteered at every school event and acted like she'd been crowned queen of recess.

Today, she'd taken up her usual post as the kickball referee, and apparently, she'd just decided my son's fate.

"What?!" I said loud enough for her and everyone else to hear, stepping closer to the field.

"He was safe, Julie! You can't call that out!" She didn't even look at me at first, just waved a hand dismissively.

"I saw it. He's out. Ball beat him."

I felt the heat creeping up my neck. Will was already trudging back toward the sidelines, head down, shoulders slumped like he'd let the whole world down. That sight flipped a switch in me—nobody was going to crush my kid's spirit!

"No way!" I said, marching up to her.
"His foot was on the base before the ball even got there. You're wrong!"

Julie finally turned, eyes narrowing.

"I call what I saw. End of story."

"End of *story?*"

"It's a kid's game JJJUUULLLIIIEEE, and *you're* screwing it up!"

Julie took a step closer to me, closing the gap. She started commenting on my parenting skills and recent weight gain. I don't remember all the words that led to the final insults, but I remember it ended with me screaming at the top of my lungs,

"You're a smoking crack whore, and a horrible mother! *Go home!*"

The playground went quiet, heads turning our way. Kids paused mid-run, their eyes wide, while a couple whispered to each other like they had front-row seats to a live show.

Somewhere in the haze, I caught a glimpse of Will staring at us, his face pale and confused.

I knew... *I went WAY too far.*

"Enough!" A new voice cut through, firm and commanding. The weight of it hit me all at once—embarrassment, guilt, anger still simmering at the surface.

I turned away, avoiding Julie's eyes, and strode toward Will. He didn't say a word as I grabbed his small, trembling fingers in mine. My face burned as I walked past the other moms, the staring kids, and the principal shaking his head.

The drive home was silent, Will staring out the window while I gripped the steering wheel too tightly.

I kept replaying it in my head—the shouting, the insults, the way we'd lost it in front of everyone.

By the time we pulled into the driveway, my stomach was in a knot of regret. I'd wanted to defend my son, but all I had done was make a fool of myself—*and him.*

Later that night, after Will was in bed, I sat on the couch with a cup of tea I didn't drink, staring at the wall. The school had called, leaving a polite but firm message about a meeting to discuss the incident.

I knew what that meant: A lecture, maybe a warning, and a whole lot of awkwardness the next time I showed my face at pickup.

And I was right. It was *exactly* what happened.

Months later, the story took an unexpected twist.
I didn't realize then how the outburst would follow me.

Later, I found out that Julie's son was on my football team.

My husband brought her and her husband to introduce the new kid on the football team and our *brand-new neighbor.*

Walking up to the back of a familiar frame, I knew before she even turned... It was Julie. Suddenly, she was everywhere—a constant reminder of my failure to keep it together.

That's the thing about emotions: They are powerful and real, but if we don't hold the reins of that wild horse, they'll run us off a cliff. And when we let ourselves ramp up to the point of losing control, we hand the enemy an open door. He slips in, turning a fleeting frustration into a lasting mess. Straining relationships, missed chances, broken pieces.

But there's a better way: **pause and give it to God.**

That's why it's so important to pause. We've all been there—feeling that heat rise in our chest, words itching to spill out, actions begging to take over...

It's human, but the Bible warns us—unchecked emotions lead us astray.

Proverbs 16:32 says, *"Better a patient person than a warrior, one with self-control than one who takes a city."*

When we pause, we take back the reins.
We stop the spiral.

We say, *"Lord, I can't do this alone, take it."*

And He does.

He calms the storm inside us, giving us clarity where there is chaos, peace where there is rage.

My emotions screamed that I'd been wronged, but they were blind to the bigger picture. The greatest thing I could've done—the greatest thing we can all do—is *pause.*

Take a breath and look at it from a biblical perspective.

Feelings are incredible—they let us laugh, cry, love—but they're not our compass. Left unchecked, they're the enemy's playground, a tool he uses to pull us off course.

Sometimes you have to pause, close your eyes, and whisper, "God, help me see this right."

Here's the truth: **Here's the truth: Your feelings are real, they're a gift—but they need a jockey—faith, wisdom, and God's word—to guide them.**

Just as Moses struck the rock, the consequences of our words can be severe. He was kept from entering the promised land.

Imagine if Moses had taken a deep breath, counted to 10, and spoken to that rock like God told him to. Instead of whacking the rock like it owed him money. Might make you laugh, but in truth, how often do we do the same thing?

One moment of letting frustration speak louder than obedience changed his entire course. When our minds are under pressure and our mouths are ready to release words of anger, we have to remember that those words carry weight.

The enemy will use those words to sow bitterness, division, and regret.

But in pausing, we not only *honor* Him, but we *protect* our future.

Victory is not found in seeing what we feel in the moment, but in allowing God's words to shape what we release.

Self-control may feel small in the moment, but it leads us to a place of peace, where anger can never take us.

Next time a battle rages in your brain, don't let the horses run wild. Pause. Ask, "Is this feeling leading me toward God or away from Him?" Then lean into His truth.

You're not powerless in the fight. With God riding alongside you, you can tame the wildest emotions and turn them into something beautiful—strength, peace, and grace. Stand tall, grab the reins. And let *Him* lead you.

Remember Moses—when he lashed out in anger and missed the promised land. And Peter, who let fear drive him to deny Jesus.

Me? I let offense turn a kid's game into a personal standoff.

But God offers us a reset.

James 1:19-20 urges us, "*...be slow to speak and slow to become angry, because human anger does not produce the righteousness that God desires.*"

Pausing isn't a weakness—it's a strength.

It's trusting that God has a better plan than our knee-jerk reactions.

Here's the kicker: When we don't pause, we're not just hurting ourselves-we're giving the enemy a foothold.

Ephesians 4:27 says, "*Do not give the devil a foothold.*"

That day with Julie, I didn't just lose control—I opened a door. My outburst built a wall between us, and then I had to face her at my son's football games, and as a neighbor.

The enemy loved that—taking a small moment and twisting it into ongoing tension and *embarrassment.*

He thrives when we're out of control, because that's when we're not leaning into God. But when we pause, we shut that door. We say, "Not today." We hand God our mess—our anger, our hurt, our fear—our offense and let Him turn it into something good. That's the power we have in Him.

So here's the challenge. Next time you feel that wild horse rearing up, whether it's a rude co-worker, a stubborn kid, or a petty argument...

Stop.
Breathe.
Pray, "God, take this."
Make it a habit.

Watch how He tames it. For me, it meant apologizing to Julie (even though I was right), apologizing, and starting over. It wasn't dramatic, but it worked. The tension faded, and I got my peace back.

You can too. *Pause.*

Give it to God.

Don't let yourself ramp up to where the enemy takes over.

Because with God, you're stronger than your emotions, and that's a victory worth claiming every single day.

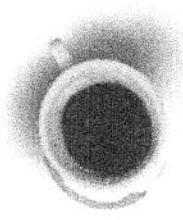

HEART CHECKS, DECLARATIONS & PRAYER

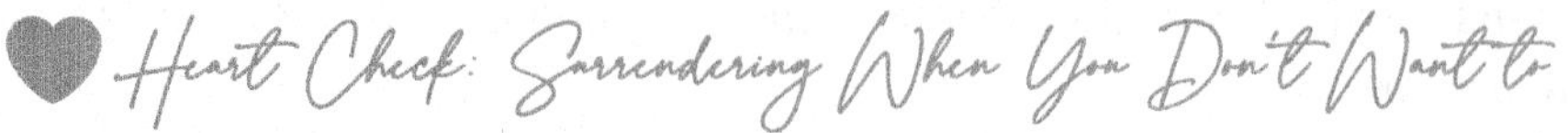

RETHINKING POINT:

Surrender isn't about feeling ready. It's about choosing trust over comfort, even when every part of you wants to hold on. God's plans often stretch us beyond what's easy, but that's where faith grows.

QUESTIONS TO ASK YOURSELF:

1. Am I resisting because I'm scared or stubborn?
2. What's the one thing I'm gripping too tightly—my plans, pride, my fears?
3. Can I take a deep breath and say, "God, I don't want to, but I'll let You have this anyway"?

REFLECTIONS:

____

____

____

____

____

____

____

____

____

God is Love

RETHINKING POINT:

The hard stuff, the fire, isn't punishment—it's God's tool to burn away what doesn't belong and polish what does.

He's not breaking you; He's making you stronger for your purpose.

QUESTIONS TO ASK YOURSELF:

1. Do I see this struggle as a dead end or a forge?
2. What might God be trying to strip away? Doubt, selfishness, distraction, lack of trust?
3. Can I shift my prayer from "Get me out" to "Shape me through this"?

REFLECTIONS:

RETHINKING POINT:

God never failed to show up in the past, and the Bible's proof is your anchor. His faithfulness then is a promise for now—your story is still unfolding, and He's already in it.

QUESTIONS TO ASK YOURSELF:

1. Have I looked at how God came through in the Scriptures, like parting the Red Sea or raising Lazarus?
2. Am I doubting He'll show up for me because I can't see it yet?
3. Can I name one time He's already been there for me and let that build my hope?

REFLECTIONS:

DECLARATION TO GOD

God, I confess that sometimes my emotions get the better of me. I let offense, frustration, and fear drive me when I should be leaning into You. Today, I give You the reins. I don't want to be controlled by my reactions—I want to be led by Your Spirit.

Teach me to pause, to breathe, and to seek You before I speak. Give me wisdom, humility, and self-control. And when I fail, remind me that You're always ready to help me start again. I trust You to calm the storm inside me.
Amen.

PRAYER

Father God,
You see it all. Every injustice, every wound, every weight I carry.
You know the frustration building inside me—the words I want to speak, the actions I want to take, the justice I want to demand.
But right now, I choose to pause.

Not because I feel strong, but because I know You are.
You are the God who sees.
The One who fights for me.
The One who never overlooks what hurts or what's unfair.

So, I bring You my anger—not to justify it, but to surrender it.
I lay down my right to react and pick up Your invitation to rest.
Help me see this moment through Your eyes—not mine.
Let me trade outrage for insight, and impulse for peace.

Father, fill me with Your Spirit.
Still, the storm inside me before I try to calm the one outside.
Make me slow to speak, slow to anger, and quick to remember:
You are not ignoring this. You are handling it.
You are my defender.
My strength.
My justice.
And I trust You.
So I pause.
And in that pause, I find You.
Amen.

GRATITUDE PROMPT

What can you thank God for? Is there a time you paused instead of reacting in anger? How did He meet you there?

Selah

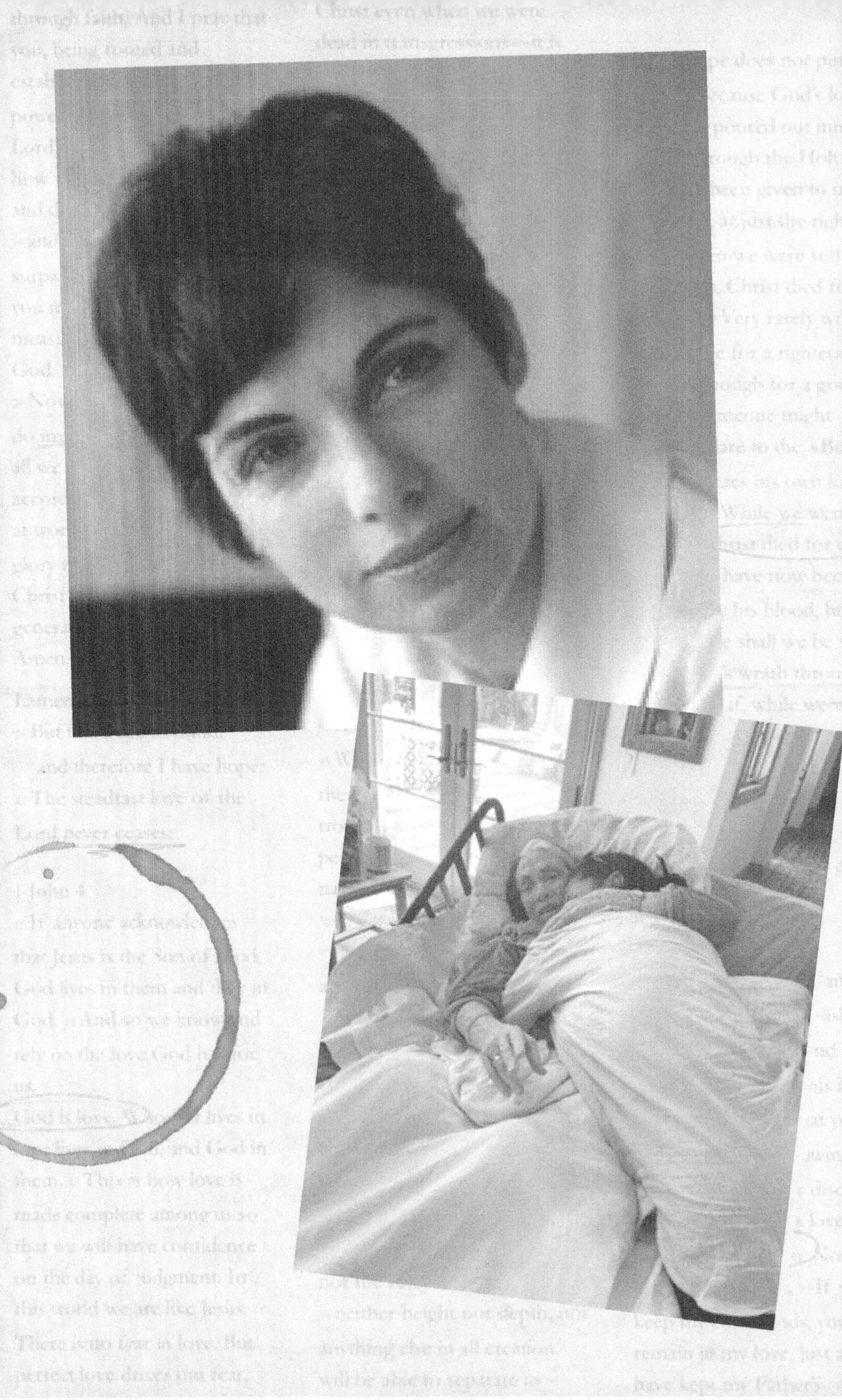

Chapter 7

The Romance Of Suffering

"The Lord does not look at the things people look at. People look at outward appearance, but the Lord looks at the heart."
1 Samuel 16:7

There exists a peculiar dance within the human soul, a strange affection some develop for the suffering they endure. Each of us carries a measure of pain, wounds carved by loss, betrayal, or the slow grind of life's trials.

For many, this suffering becomes more than a burden; it transforms into a badge, a price paid in full, a piece of their identity.

They cling to it, not because it *comforts* them, but because it's *familiar.*

Their whole life can be defined by one incident, a single moment, or a series of events that anchor them, leaving them stuck gazing into the past.

My mom carried a shadow that never left her, a wound from her childhood where abuse etched itself deep into her identity. She was little when it happened, defenseless against the cruelty that stole her innocence. And though the years piled on, she never got past it.

That pain became her identity, the lens through which she saw everything—a constant echo from when she was little. It colored every conversation, every decision. It wasn't just a memory; it was a tether, pulling her back to that broken place, and it affected her whole life.

When I was little, she would sit me down often and tell me matter-of-factly that she didn't want to live with the memory of her childhood, so she was going to commit suicide. She did this out of love, so I wouldn't blame myself, unaware of the damage it would cause.

As a child hearing those words, I would panic, grabbing a blanket, a pillow, and my favorite stuffed animal—a worn-out bear with one eye missing. I would set up in front of her room every night, sleeping in front of her door, determined to keep her alive.

I scrambled to tell a funny joke or dig up something amusing—anything to make her laugh—because I knew I had to keep her here.

It was *my desperate mission* to pull her from the edge, *a weight I carried without question.*

When the nights ended, we would start the day, every day, pretty much the same in our house on a hill. Mom shuffling around the kitchen, her eyes puffy from not sleeping well.

She'd pour her coffee, sigh, and begin talking with that familiar line: "Well, when I was little...." And just like that, she'd share bits of her sad stories from being a kid, times when she felt so lost and alone that she thought about not being here anymore.

As her little girl, I'd sit there at the table, my cereal getting soggy, wishing I could hug away all that hurt, but I was just too small to fix something so big.

She'd sometimes cry, her shoulders shaking like leaves in the wind, and it broke my heart because right there in front of her was me, her little girl. Someone who loved her with all her might, even if her own mom hadn't shown her that kind of love. I knew I could.

Every morning and every night was the same, I'd curl up on the floor right in front of her door, sleeping but always listening, always staring at the popcorn ceiling, wondering if tonight she was going to need me.

Night after night, it became my spot, so much so that I started thinking my own room down the hall was just for stacking my clothes in messy piles, dolls and shirts jumbled together. While my real place was here, like a little guard dog, ready to jump up and help.

In my little girl's eyes, I was holding her here, one morning and one night at a time.

By the seventh grade, that task grew too great. The years of holding her up, of being a lifeline, pressed down until I couldn't breathe. One night, the darkness swallowed me too.

I tried to take my own life—not out of weakness, but because the burden outweighed my strength. This isn't a story that makes me a victim: it's just a fact of my past, a chapter that shaped me, but doesn't *own* me.

Most of us carry a sad story, a wound, a loss, or a reason we're tempted to keep looking over our shoulder. But there comes a point when God causes us to lift our eyes and see that **His plans are ahead, not behind.**

Life is not meant to be lived in yesterday's shadow, but in the light of His promises. Moving forward isn't just for our sake; it's for the people we love and *those who need us whole.*

We are more than our pain, more than our past, because Christ has created us for a future filled with hope. To stay stuck in sorrow is to overlook who we are in Him, but when you walk in faith, you honor the one who made us new.

But *only* you can make that *choice.*

Our purpose is never limited by our past. He turned a murderer named Moses into a compassionate leader, a coward named Gideon into a hero, and He can do amazing things in your life too.

Those who have hurt you in the past cannot continue to hurt you now. The only power they have is the power *you* give them.

When I think about my mom's story, here's the heartbreak: She had all the love of a great mom, but her childhood pain blocked her from living in the fullness of who God created her to be.

She never lived the life God wanted for her because she never gave her pain to God. She kept it for herself, clutching it like a twisted treasure, as if letting go would unravel who she was.

I carried pain until it broke me, but then I chose another way—I gave it to God. I laid it at His feet, raw and heavy, and walked away, never looking back. It wasn't easy.

And it's also not a choice you will likely make only once. For me, it was a choice I had to make daily until one day when I laid it at God's feet once more, and I didn't have the need to pick it up again.

The Bible promises trials, not comfort, but it also offers peace if we choose it. Where my mom kept her suffering as a twisted keepsake, I surrendered mine, and that release let me step into a life *unburdened by yesterday.*

Her story stayed a monument to pain, mine a testament to letting go.

Contrast Jackie to Job, a man who faced unimaginable suffering, yet found a way to release it to God. Job lost *everything*—his wealth, his children, his health—reduced to sitting in ashes, scraping sores with broken pottery.

The pain was excruciating, and for a time, he questioned, wrestling with why such hardship was happening. But Job didn't let it define him forever.

When God spoke, revealing His sovereignty over all creation, Job chose to surrender his anguish, saying, *"I know that you can do all things; no purpose of Yours will be thwarted."* (Job 42:2)

By giving it to God, He opened the door to restoration—a life filled with doubled blessings, new children, and years of peace. Job's story proves the power of *release.*

God promises we will have trials. Jesus Himself said, *"I have told you all this so that you may have peace in me. Here on earth, you will have many trials and sorrows."* (John 16:33).

Yet He follows with hope: *"But take heart! I have overcome the world."* Trouble and tribulation, that's a guarantee, but *"you may have peace"*—shows you you have a choice. Peace is possible, but it's not automatic.

It's a choice—not made to be easy. It's hard, an active decision we must work toward, stepping out of the mire of our pain to claim it. The Bible says in 1 Pete 5:7, *"Cast all your anxiety on Him because He cares for you."*

It's completely understandable that sometimes we can get stuck. Stuck in our trauma, stuck in the bitterness, stuck in the pain, the offense, the disappointment.

We're just stuck, and that's a heavy place to be. I'm not here to dismiss the pain, nor am I minimizing the suffering or trauma you've endured. Those feelings are real, and they *matter.*

I don't say this lightly, but I'm gonna say it again because it's so, so important, but *happiness is a choice,* a *conscious effort* to refuse watering the seeds of doubt planted by the enemy.

It means taking every thought captive, as in 2 Corinthians 10:5; *"We demolish arguments and every pretension that sets itself up against the knowledge of God, and we take captive every thought to make it obedient to Christ."*

We HAVE to evaluate every thought, every seed the enemy plants. To guard our minds, stop the enemy at the gate. Does that thought bring life or death? Does it give me life and life abundantly? If the answer is not yes, train yourself to *uproot* it and *discard* it.

Put on praise music, listen to a good speaker. Put it at God's feet even if it takes 10,000 times. If not for your own sake, do it for those who love you. Do it for the people you want to see living full lives without the burden of your pain.

Stop the repeat of "I just can't get better." "My divorce, my childhood, my mom or dad, my ...." Give it to God. You are never meant to carry that burden alone. Choose a full life!!!

There comes a time when we need to shift our focus and make what Jesus did FOR us bigger than what anyone has done TO us.

This isn't about ignoring the hurt:
It's about choosing to let the hope, healing, and love He offers outweigh the wounds we've carried.

You're not alone in this, and He gives us grace for the journey forward.

My mom, though, couldn't—or wouldn't—let go. Instead, she let it define her, a pillar of pain standing where faith could have brought healing. Her childhood became her whole story, a mental treadmill she couldn't step off.

Her life became a testament to what happens when we hold suffering too close, refusing the freedom God offers to those who lay it at His feet.

If *life* is what you choose, lay everything else at His feet and walk away!

My mom and I never really knew how to spend time together. I loved her, and she loved me, but there was always this unspoken awkwardness, a quiet wall we couldn't quite climb.

We drifted through the years like that, connected but distant, until early dementia crept into her life, stealing her sharpness but, unexpectedly, giving me something back.

At first, I visited out of guilt, a single trip to ease my conscience, but I was there several times a week, drawn by the woman she was becoming.

In that haze of dementia, she shed the weight of whatever had held her back and reverted to who I believe God always meant her to be.

She'd laugh at everything, pure, bubbling giggles over the smallest things, every moment a joke, every glance a spark of innocence. It was as if the veil lifted, and I saw her, not as the mom shaped by life's struggles, but as the joyful, unburdened woman that God had crafted.

I stopped mourning the life we should have lived, and started cherishing the life we had now, right there in front of me.

Now she's in heaven, free in a way she rarely was here, and I know when I join her, we'll be best friends; every missed childhood moment is waiting to unfold in eternity.

But here's the gift: If you can *let go* of the regrets, that freedom, that laughter, *doesn't have to wait.*

It's a blessing we can utilize on earth, even now.

HEART CHECKS, DECLARATIONS & PRAYER

RETHINKING POINT:

Dwelling in the past keeps you trapped in a cycle of pain. Moving forward has to start with giving that burden to God. He doesn't want you stuck replaying the bad; He's ready to take it and guide you into something new.

QUESTIONS TO ASK YOURSELF:

1. Do I ruminate about bad things that have happened in my past, or do I allow myself to move forward?
2. Do I hold on to the pain, or do I give it to God and step into healing?
3. What hang-ups or fears might be keeping you from living out God's vision for your life?

REFLECTIONS:

God is Love

RETHINKING POINT:

Holding onto pain can feel like a twisted comfort, but it blocks the life God has waiting for you. Surrendering it to Him doesn't erase what happened—it frees you to live beyond it, trusting He's bigger than your history.

QUESTIONS TO ASK YOURSELF:

1. Do I hold onto the pain of the past, or do I give it to God and move forward?
2. Do I try to have the life God has for me, or am I convinced I'm too damaged to claim it?
3. Would people around me say I ruminated and often talk about the pain of the past?

REFLECTIONS:

____

____

____

____

____

____

____

RETHINKING POINT:

The past might leave scars, but God sees you as a work in progress, not a write-off. Letting go of the "damaged forever" label means embracing the future He's crafting—one where your story honors Him, not your wounds.

QUESTIONS TO ASK YOURSELF:

1. Do I dwell in my past and see myself as damaged forever, or do I move forward with God?
2. Do I pursue the life He's offering, or am I letting pain define me instead of His purpose?
3. Can I commit not to ruminate on the past?

REFLECTIONS:

____

____

____

____

____

____

____

____

DECLARATION TO GOD

God, I don't want to be defined by my wounds.
I don't want to live anchored to the pain of the past.
Today, I choose to hand You what I've carried far too long.
The memory. The fear. The bitterness. The grief.
I won't cling to pain like a trophy anymore.
You are bigger than my past.
You are the Healer of every broken place.
You are writing a new story with my life.
And I believe You are not finished with me yet.

PRAYER

Father,
You know the heaviness I carry—the pain I've clung to and the lies I've believed. I don't want to stay stuck, replaying what hurt me over and over again. I want freedom. I want healing. Help me to give You everything I've held back. Take the fear, the bitterness, the guilt, the ache. Heal the places no one else sees. Teach me to trust You with my story—even the hard parts. I believe You can redeem anything. Even me. Even this. Amen.

GRATITUDE PROMPT

What am I grateful for today? Consider the blessings, both big and small, that God has placed in your life.

____

____

____

____

____

____

Selah

through faith. And I pray that
you, being rooted and
established in love, may have
power, together with all the
Lord's holy people, to grasp
how wide and long and high
and deep is the love of Ch

Christ even when we were
dead in transgressions—it is
by grace you have been saved.
6 And God raised us up with
Christ and seated us with him
in the heavenly realms in

5 And hope does not put
shame, because God's lo
has been poured out into
hearts through the Holy

made complete among us so
that we will have confidence
on the day of judgment: In
this world we are like Jesus. 18
There is no fear in love. But
perfect love drives out fear,

nor life, neither angels nor
demons, neither the present
nor the future, nor any p
39 neither height nor depth, nor
anything else in all creation,
will be able to separate us

yourselves to be my disci
9 As the Father has love
so have I loved you. Now
remain in my love. 10 If y
keep my commandments, you
remain in my love, just a
have kept my Father's

Don't I Count?

"Are not five sparrows sold for two pennies?
Yet not one of them is forgotten by God.
Indeed, the very hairs of your head are all numbered.
Don't be afraid; You are worth more than many sparrows."
Luke 12:6-7

I woke up to the sound of Kylie giggling in the kitchen—her tiny hands no doubt fumbling through cereal boxes or juice cartons, plotting a crumb-filled surprise with the determination of a raccoon in a pantry. I padded downstairs, groggy and curious, and there she was.

Standing on a stool, her pixie hair dusted in flour, was my Kylie.

A plate of slightly charred pancakes—possibly a pancake, possibly a science experiment—waited proudly on the counter.

"*Happy Mother's Day, Mommy!*" she squealed, throwing her arms around me, smacking me with that fierce little-girl love that's all elbows and syrup and devotion. You could feel it deep down in your soul.

Which is why this next part stings a little.

That same grinning pancake fairy? I would accidentally leave her behind hours later at Soup Plantation.

Let me explain.

It was Mother's Day, and I'd planned a hiking adventure with all five of my kids—including the baby I was wearing like a kangaroo pouch. Kylie, my 8-year-old firecracker, was bouncing with excitement.

We hit the trail, and the kids took off like a joyful stampede—muddy, laughing, full of life. The older ones helped the littler ones, the baby napping against my chest, and for a second, I thought: *Look at us.*

We're one wholesome snack commercial away from perfect.

We hiked, we climbed, we splashed through puddles. It was chaotic, beautiful, and muddy—exactly how family should be.

Eventually, tired and ravenous, we headed to Soup Plantation.
(RIP, dear carb haven. We didn't know how good we had it.)

Each kid grabbed a tray and executed their own vision of lunch. One made a salad mountain, one took only muffins, and Kylie curated a masterpiece of cornbread, pudding, macaroni, and joy.
It was loud. It was messy. It was ours.

As we were leaving, Kylie said, "Bathroom break!"

I nodded automatically, distracted by someone spilling frozen yogurt on their shoe and the baby rooting for a feed. I assumed she was right behind us.

We herded the others out to the parking lot, strapped them in, and I turned the key—

Nothing.
Just a sad little wheeze.
Dead battery.

I whispered a quick prayer, smacked the steering wheel, tried again—and miraculously, it roared to life.

"Everyone in, let's go!" I shouted, already picturing the baby losing it and the older ones turning feral.

We peeled out like a clown car fleeing the apocalypse. The engine sputtered and groaned like it was on its last breath, and suddenly, no one had anything to say.

The car was quiet. Too quiet.
No arguing over snacks. No one asking how long until we get home.

Not even a single, blessed "Mooooommmm."

The silence wasn't peaceful—it was cautious. Like, even the kids understood we were living on borrowed battery life and hope. Eric stared ahead, white knuckling the steering wheel like it owed him money.

I kept one eye on the dashboard and the other on the baby, who had mercifully passed out in the carrier, drooling on my chest like a warm, sticky paperweight.

I think we all knew: If the car stopped again, we were going to have to live off macaroni and moral support until AAA found us.

So, we held our breath and rolled through traffic lights like we were sneaking past a sleeping dragon. And just when the car stopped coughing and started humming—just when I thought we might make it home without a nervous breakdown—I decided to lighten the mood.

"Alright, team," I said, trying to sound breezy but probably sounding like I was auditioning for a local news segment called *Mothers on the Verge*.

"What was your favorite part of the day?"

The answers came quickly and cheerfully.
"The mud!"
"The muffins!"
"The giant leaf I found that looked like a pancake!"

We were coming back to life. We were going to be okay.

Then I turned to Kylie's seat.

"Ky, your turn. What was your favorite part?" *Silence.*

I looked over my shoulder.

"Kylie?" I said again, still smiling. *Nothing.*

That's when a strange, sinking sensation hit my stomach. Like the last bite of yogurt before you realize it expired three days ago.

I twisted in my seat.
Her spot was empty.
Empty.

"KYLIE'S NOT IN THE CAR!" I shrieked, my voice cracking in sheer horror. Eric slammed on the brakes so hard the baby farted in protest.

I fumbled for my phone while mentally fast-forwarding through every worst-case scenario imaginable. I could already see her—alone, scared, wandering the salad bar, whispering, "Mommy?" to strangers in the soup line.

I dialed Soup Plantation with shaking fingers.

"*Hi, yes—um—I think I left my daughter there?*" I asked, trying not to sound like the woman who had just driven off with 80% of her children but forgot one, like an umbrella left behind in a booth.

The manager paused. "Uh... I'm looking around now... No kids here."

Cue full-blown *panic.*
My heart *dropped* to my knees.

We flipped a U-turn (questionable legality, zero regrets) and tore back to the restaurant.

Please, please let her be okay.
Please let her know we didn't mean it.
Please let her still love me and make weird pancakes in the morning.

And then—I saw her.
There she was.

Sitting on a bench, legs swinging, hands folded like a miniature, betrayed dignitary waiting for her security detail to return.

She had already written two TED Talks in her head about bad parenting.

Her little head turned as we pulled in.

And those eyes… *oh, those eyes.*

Not scared. Not tearful. Just burning with pure: ***How Dare You?!***

A mixture of betrayal, sass, and the kind of energy that could flatten a village.

She climbed into the car without a word.

Crossed her arms. Turned her head to the window.

We drove the rest of the way home in what I can only describe as shame-filled silence. Not because of the battery. Not because of the road.

Because of her.
Because I had forgotten my pancake fairy.
And she *knew* it.

When we got home, I sent the boys off to build something or break something—whichever struck their spirits—and unbuckled the baby with one arm while reaching for Kylie with the other.

She didn't *move.*

I knelt beside her, still squatting half-sideways with a baby latched to me like an angry barnacle, and whispered, "Sweetheart... will you come talk to me for a minute?"

Still no words. Just the arms. Crossed tighter now.

But she followed me inside, walking like she was starring in a courtroom drama, and I was about to be sentenced.

We sat on the couch, the baby now wedged between us like a sticky, drooling referee.

Kylie's face was a thundercloud—dark, brewing, but not yet pouring. Just low, rumbly betrayal with a hint of *"I'm still deciding whether I'll let this define my childhood."*

I took a deep breath.

"Kylie," I said softly, "I am so, so sorry. I thought you were right behind me. I would never leave you on purpose."

She stared straight ahead. And then—without looking at me—she said it.

"You forgot me."

My heart cracked right down the middle. I felt every ounce of her tiny hurt. The way it lodged itself in her chest like it had been waiting for proof that maybe, just maybe, she didn't matter as much as the others. And I had handed it to her.

Tears pricked the corners of my eyes. "I didn't mean to, baby. I messed up. But you matter to me so much. *You count, Kylie.*"

She finally looked at me.

And whispered the sentence that wrecked me:
"But you did forget me. Don't I count?"
There it was.

That deep little sentence that lives in all of us, tucked between our ribs like a splinter: *Don't I count?*

We don't always ask it out loud. Sometimes we whisper it in silence. Sometimes we throw it across the room in the middle of a fight.

Sometimes we carry it for decades. But it's there.

In every heart, aching to be seen.
To matter.

I pulled her in close, baby and all. It was a clumsy, sideways, emotionally snotty hug, but I held her like I was trying to squeeze that lie right out of her bones.

"You count so much, Kylie. You're unforgettable. I am so sorry I made you feel otherwise."

She sniffled. Nodded. Let her arms go limp against me.

The storm didn't fully break—but the sky cracked just enough for grace to come through.

And that moment? That was the miracle of the day.

Not the pancake. Not the hike. Not even the resurrection of the Soup Plantation parking lot battery.

It was the chance to go back.
To say the thing.
To rewrite the lie with truth.

Because sometimes love doesn't look like getting it right the first time. Sometimes it looks like turning around, racing back, and sitting on a couch next to a furious eight-year-old who just needs to know she was worth remembering.

And I will never, ever forget that again.

Sometimes we feel like the one left behind. Like the world moved on without us. Like our voice didn't matter enough to be missed. But when love returns—when someone sees us, really sees us—it rewrites the lie.

So, I'll never forget that day. The hiking, the muffins, the miracle of the car restarting.

But most of all, I'll remember the fierce little girl who taught me how much being seen matters.

And trust me—she'll never let me forget her again.

When we feel overlooked, left behind, unseen—*He sees us.* He counts every hair on our heads. He calls us by name. Not one of us is forgotten. Not one.

This is the God who never leaves *anyone* behind. We have to remember this, so we don't take the emotions we feel and make them who we are.

You are not your emotions. It's important that we reflect biblically on ego, emotion, and surrender.

It's crucial that we learn to identify our emotions—but not become them. Emotions are real, yes, but they are not permanent. They are *not* your identity.

They pass like clouds in the sky. The trouble comes when we cling to them, define ourselves by them, and let them shape our beliefs about who we are.

To take control of your emotions, you must first understand: they are temporary. You don't need to repress them or push them into the shadows of your subconscious.

But you also don't need to invite them to live in your heart rent-free.

As 2 Corinthians 10:5 reminds us, we are called to "*...take every thought captive to make it obedient to Christ.*"

But it doesn't end there. To truly master your emotions, you must also understand your ego—your self-identity. Ego is often built from the meanings we assign to life's events.

Some moments—like being left behind or rejected—cut deeper than others. But it's our interpretation of these moments that shapes us.

For example, you say something embarrassing in a group, and now you identify as someone who "always says the wrong thing".

Your paycheck is smaller than you'd like, and now you carry the identity of someone who is "failing" or "not enough".

You were once left behind—maybe literally, at a place like Soup Plantation —and now you believe you're "invisible" or "unwanted".

But here's the truth: these moments don't define you. *Only* God does.

Romans 12:2 says, "*Do not conform to the pattern of this world, but be transformed by the renewing of your mind.*" That means we must actively separate our identity from fleeting feelings and mistaken beliefs. (I've used this verse a couple of times in this book; it's that important!)

That's because emotions are not your identity.

Few people stop to ask: Where did this feeling come from? Often, it's a thought—random or triggered by memory—that we cling to and begin to identify with. But emotions are just that: feelings.

Not *facts.* Not *truth.* Not the essence of *who you are.*

You are not "stressed." You are feeling stressed. You are not "sad." You are experiencing sadness. These distinctions matter deeply.

Your feelings are like guests—they may visit, but they were never meant to take up residence.

As Psalm 30:5 reminds us, "*Weeping may endure for a night, but joy comes in the morning.*"

One helpful practice I've found was in this book called *The Sedona Method*, by Hale Dwoskin. It offers a process for letting go of emotional burdens.

While the method is not explicitly biblical, it can be adapted as a tool to draw nearer to God.

Here's a Christ-centered approach based on the method:

Observe the emotion:

Name what you're feeling without judgment.
Don't attach it to your identity.
Pray: "Lord, reveal the root of this feeling. Show me the lie I've believed."

Label it truthfully:

Instead of "I am anxious," say, "I am feeling anxious today."
Remember: Your heart is not your home for anxiety.

"*Cast all your anxiety on Him because He cares for you.*" (1 Peter 5:7)

Let it go—ask yourself:

Could I allow this feeling to be here for now?
Could I let it go?
Could I welcome it and release it into God's hands?

Then ask:

Would I give this to God?
When?

Do this prayerfully and repeatedly until your heart begins to soften.

"Come to me, all who are weary and burdened, and I will give you rest." (Matthew 11:28)

Some wounds feel too deep, some emotions feel too overwhelming. For those, walk through this process closely with Jesus. Visualize yourself laying the burden at His feet.

Picture Him beside you. Hear Him say, *"I will never leave you nor forsake you."* (Deuteronomy 31:6)

Feel the comfort of releasing your pain into the hands that were pierced for your healing.

"He heals the brokenhearted and binds up their wounds." (Psalm 147:3)

You are not the worst thing that has ever happened to you. Nor are you the greatest. You are beloved by God, refined in fire, not destroyed by it.

Let every hardship form compassion in you, not bitterness.
Let every wound become a place where grace shines through.

"Consider it pure joy... whenever you face trials... because you know that the testing of your faith produces perseverance." (James 1:2-3)

Train your ego not to defend, not to compare, not to inflate itself, but to rejoice with others, forgive quickly, and reflect the heart of Christ.

You can overcome.

Every trial you have faced is proof that your emotions are not eternal. They do not define you. God does. He is faithful.

He will not let you drown in waters deeper than you can swim.

"When you pass through the waters, I will be with you; and through the rivers, they shall not overwhelm you." (Isaiah 43:2)

So let go. Breathe. Surrender.

You are not your fear.
You are not your guilt.
You are not your past.
You are loved.
You are growing.

You are being made new.

HEART CHECKS, DECLARATIONS & PRAYER

RETHINKING POINT:

Your emotions are real, but they are not your identity

"Feelings are visitors, not permanent residents. You are not what you feel—you are who God says you are."

QUESTIONS TO ASK YOURSELF:

1. Am I labeling myself based on what I feel today?
2. Am I giving more attention to my feelings than to God's truth?
3. Have I invited God into my emotional life, or am I trying to manage it alone?

REFLECTIONS:

God is Love

Heart Check: Your Truth & Ego

RETHINKING POINT:

Your ego forms from interpretation, not truth.

"What happened to you is not who you are. The meaning you attach to it either builds your ego or surrenders it to God."

Romans 12:3, *"Do not think of yourself more highly than you ought, but rather think of yourself with sober judgment..."*

QUESTIONS TO ASK YOURSELF:

1. Am I building a story around my pain that God never wrote?
2. Is my ego protecting me from humility or healing?
3. Do I seek validation more than transformation?

REFLECTIONS:

____

____

____

____

____

____

____

____

RETHINKING POINT:

You can lay it down at the feet of Jesus.

"You don't have to carry what Jesus already offered to hold. Surrender doesn't mean weakness—it means trust."

Matthew 11:28, *"Come to me, all you who are weary and burdened, and I will give you rest."*

QUESTIONS TO ASK YOURSELF:

1. Am I labeling myself based on what I feel today?
2. Am I giving more attention to my feelings than to God's truth?
3. Have I invited God into my emotional life, or am I trying to manage it alone?

REFLECTIONS:

DECLARATION TO GOD

I am not forgotten.
You see me, God.
Even when I feel invisible, left behind, or overlooked, You never take Your eyes off me. I matter to You. I am chosen, cherished, and remembered. You will never leave me behind. I am held by a love that never forgets.

PRAYER

Lord,
Sometimes I feel like the one left behind—unseen, unheard, unimportant. But I know that's not the truth. You are the God who leaves the ninety-nine for the one. You never forget, never overlook, never abandon. Thank You for counting me, for loving me in my mess, my silence, and my sorrow. Rewrite the lies I've believed with Your truth. And help me, in turn, to see others who feel unseen. Let me reflect Your fierce and faithful love. Amen.

GRATITUDE PROMPT

Today, I'm thankful for:

Selah

The Easter Bunny

"I have come that they may have life, and have it to the full."
John 10:10

Rett loved Easter. It wasn't just the bright colors of the dyed Easter eggs or the thrill of the hunt that drew him in. It was the promise of something sweet, something special. To Rett, Easter was a day of joy, a celebration made just for him—a day Grandma came to visit, always with *something special.*

One year, Grandma came with something that stopped Rett in his tracks.

In Patty's arms was the biggest Easter bunny Rett had ever seen, almost as tall as he was, a towering giant wrapped in gleaming foil. Its ears stretched high above his head, and its round belly was wider than his little arms could hug. He grabbed those ears with both hands, hefting it up, marveling at its size.

This wasn't just a bunny; it was a mountain of chocolate, a treasure he could barely carry. He could already taste it—rich, creamy, melt-in-your-mouth goodness**, the best thing he'd ever eaten.** His mouth watered just thinking about it. But Grandma, wise and steady, put a hand on his shoulder. "Hold on, Rett," she said. "Breakfast first, then the Easter egg hunt. The bunny comes at the end."

Rett's heart thudded, his little body wrung with impatience, but he nodded, dragging that massive bunny by the ears to the table. It thumped against the door, nearly as big as he was, a constant tease as he choked down the scrambled eggs, the orange juice, the toast, and the crispy bacon.

He barely tasted any of it, poking at his plate. He didn't even enjoy the breakfast that only came twice a year. All he could picture was biting into the giant bunny and how amazing it was going to be.

The Easter egg hunt felt like a long marathon. Out in the yard, Rett lugged the bunny along at first, its foil glinting in the grass. It was so big it slowed him down, bumping his knees, so Grandma finally took it inside. "Keep going, Rett, it will be worth it," she called.

He tried to focus, grabbing eggs here and there while his siblings ran in the grass and laughed. Normally, Rett loved it, but not today. His mind was focused on the colossal bunny.

It was his prize. His dream. This giant was his *destiny.*

Family chatter, the warm breeze, the bright day—none of it sank in. That chocolate bunny was his sole thought. Finally, the hunt ended. "Okay, Rett," Grandma said, holding the bunny. "You can have the bunny now."

Rett raced over, grabbed those huge ears, and chomped down. But instead of a flood of rich chocolate, it was hollow—just a thin shell that cracked and fell apart. No sweetness, no fullness.

Tears welled up as he stared at the empty bite. "It's *hollow!*"

Empty, hollow, futile, *nothing.*

This is the life of many—hands grasping for sweet things that melt away.

Possessions. Experiences. Power. Pleasure.

It's the chase of the wind, the reaching for vapor, a hunger that's never satisfied. Without the Holy Spirit, life is hollow.

Think about it: No matter how big the chocolate bunny is, it's still hollow inside. What looks full, promising, and delightful turns out to be fragile and breakable when you bite into it. That's life without God—shiny on the outside, but empty at the core.

This is the myth we've been sold: If I get more, I will be more.

But that is a *lie.*
Self-worth and net worth are not the same thing.
Your *value* is not determined by your *valuables.*

The truth? God reminds us that the most valuable things in life are not "things" at all. "*For what will it profit a man if he gains the whole world and forfeits his soul?*" (Mark 8:36)

A hollow life is spent running after what fades: money, fun, even health. They come and go, slipping through your fingers like sand. And when they do, you're left with nothing solid, no foundation, no anchor.

Without God, life feels like chasing shadows.

But a whole life—one centered on godly things—is unshakable. The treasures of the Spirit are eternal: Love, joy, peace, patience, kindness, goodness, faithfulness, gentleness, self-control. These are not subject to the stock market, your health report, or the shifting opinions of others. They endure *forever.*

Esau's story in Genesis is a sobering picture of this truth. As the firstborn, he held a birthright—a sacred inheritance that carried God's promise and blessing. It was priceless, a gift beyond measure.

By birthright, he stood in the direct line of Abraham, positioned to inherit not just land and livestock, but the covenant blessing of God's chosen people. His future was tied to heaven's promises.

But one day, coming in from the fields, all Esau could feel was hunger.

The hunt had drained him. His body was tired, his throat dry, his stomach gnawed with emptiness. As he staggered into camp, the smell of stew drifted through the air—lentils simmering, bread warming beside the fire. Jacob stood nearby, stirring the pot, watching his brother weaken.

"Let me eat some of that red stew, for I am exhausted," Esau pleaded. His voice was heavy, more of a demand than a request.

Jacob saw his moment. "Sell me your birthright now."

The words should have jolted Esau to his senses. The birthright was his identity, his privilege, his future. But at that moment, Esau's appetite shouted louder than his calling.

"I am about to die," he said, exaggerating his condition. "Of what use is a birthright to me?"

With that, he swore an oath, handing away his inheritance for a single meal.

Can you imagine it? Jacob passing him the bread, Esau lifting the bowl, gulping down the stew in greedy mouthfuls. The hunger eased. The craving silenced. The bowl scraped clean. But with every bite, something *immeasurable* slipped from his hands.

And then it was gone. The pot was empty, the fire burned low, and Esau sat full—but hollow. He had satisfied his stomach but forfeited his soul. The Scriptures sum it up with painful simplicity: "*Thus Esau despised his birthright.*" (Genesis 25:34)

Hebrews 12:16-17 tells us Esau later sought the blessing with tears, but he could not undo what was done. A choice made in haste left a wound that could not be reversed. His story has echoed for centuries as a warning: *Don't trade the eternal for the immediate.*

Now contrast Esau with Jesus in the wilderness.
Forty days of fasting, hunger gnawing at Him, temptation pressing from

every side. The devil offered bread—instant relief, immediate satisfaction—but Jesus did not yield. *"Man shall not live on bread alone, but on every word that comes from the mouth of God."* (Matthew 4:4)

Unlike Esau, Jesus saw beyond the moment. He refused the temporary and clung to the eternal. His obedience secured a victory no meal could ever provide.

That's the danger of living for the temporary. We chase what looks shiny or comforting, but in the end, it leaves us emptier than before. Esau's choice whispers a lesson to every one of us: *Don't trade your eternal inheritance for temporary satisfaction.*

How often do we do the same?
We reach for status, thinking it will secure our identity.
We chase experiences, hoping they will give our lives meaning.
We cling to possessions, believing they will anchor our worth.

But none of these last. They fade, break, rust, or vanish. Only God satisfies.

"Do not store up for yourselves treasures on earth, where moth and rust destroy, and where thieves break in and steal. But store up for yourselves treasures in heaven... for where your treasure is, there your heart will be also." (Matthew 6:19-21)

A hollow life is fragile, but a whole life in Christ is full.
Full of purpose. Full of peace. Full of joy that no one can take away. *"And this is the promise that He made to us—eternal life."* (1 John 2:25)

So, what are you hungry for today? What stew is the enemy holding under your nose, hoping you'll give up something eternal for something that won't last?

Don't fall for it. Don't trade your birthright for a bowl.

God has already given you *"...an inheritance that cannot spoil, perish, or fade"* (1 Peter 1:4). What looks hollow in this world, God can make whole in Him.

Choose the fullness of Christ over the emptiness of the world. And watch how He takes what feels futile and fills it with meaning that lasts forever.

A hollow life is running after things that come and go, and you're left with nothing solid.

Without God, it feels empty.

But when you focus on godly things, you're left with something real that sticks around forever.

Worldly things fade, but God *doesn't.*

Esau had a birthright, a huge blessing worth everything. But he got hungry, so he focused on short-term desire; he didn't consider the long-term value of his birthright.

Driven by immediate hunger, he focused on a single bowl of stew, that bowl stole his identity, who God created him to be.

He traded it all away for one quick meal.
When he ate, it filled his stomach, but it left his life hollow.
He chased one single thing and lost the bigger prize.

Rett's bunny ears were his stew—big, shiny, and hollow. He'd been so zeroed in, he missed the feast on his plate, the hunt with his siblings, the sun on his face, the day with his grandma. His goal was a bust, and he'd let everything else slip by.

But here's the fire in this story—God doesn't want us stuck on hollow things. He's got a full life waiting.

John 10:10 says, *"I have come that they may have life, and have it to the full."*

God Himself hides Easter eggs in our days, little joys He waits for us to find. Warm hugs, a good laugh, a bright morning.

Rett almost missed them all, chasing those ears. Don't get this wrong—God's not about laziness. He calls us to run hard, to set goals, to chase dreams.

Press on toward your goals, but don't get so tunnel-visioned that you stumble over the treasures He's tucked along the way.

Rett wiped his tears and stood up. He loudly proclaimed he wouldn't waste Easter again.

The bunny flopped, but God didn't.

Life's not one empty ear—it's a hunt full of surprises, waiting for you to find them.

God has such a great plan for you.

Don't let things pass you by while waiting for something bigger to happen.

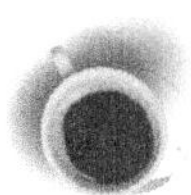

HEART CHECKS, DECLARATIONS & PRAYER

RETHINKING POINT:

A hollow life comes from running after stuff that shines but fades: money, status, quick thrills, leaving you empty. The glitter wears off. Godly things fill you up for keeps, not just the moment.

QUESTIONS TO ASK YOURSELF:

1. Am I chasing things that look good but leave me feeling flat?
2. What's one worldly thing I'm hooked on that really feeds my soul? Can I turn my eyes to something God cares about instead, like kindness or trust?
3. Can I tell the difference between things that are temporary and eternal?

REFLECTIONS:

God is Love

Heart Check: Seeking Worldly Over Godly

RETHINKING POINT:

Worldly stuff promises a buzz, new gadgets, applause, and a fat wallet. But it's a leaky bucket: Godly stuff, like peace or helping others, holds water forever. You've got to pick what you're pouring into.

QUESTIONS TO ASK YOURSELF:

1. Do I spend more time hunting for cash or cool things than I do with God?
2. What's one worldly thing I lean on that always lets me down?
3. Could I swap an hour of scrolling for an hour of prayer and see what sticks?

REFLECTIONS:

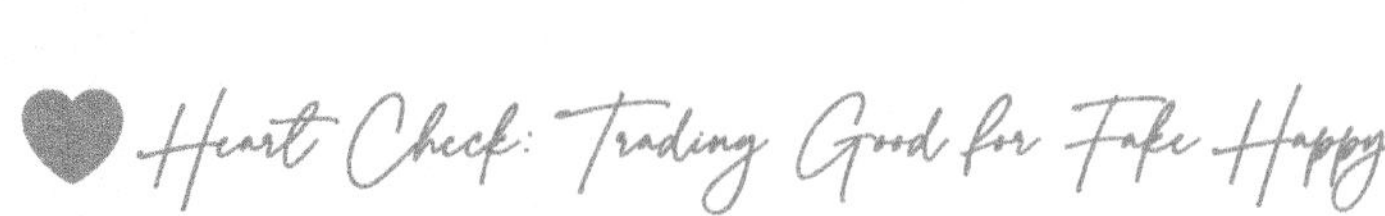

RETHINKING POINT:

It's easy to trade what's good for you, like rest, real love, or faith in what you think will make you happy, like more stuff or being seen. Knowing the difference is key to spotting it before it hooks you.

QUESTIONS TO ASK YOURSELF:

1. Am I grabbing at things I think will cheer me up but leave me tired? What's one good thing? Time with God? Do I seek something shiny or shallow, feeding my flesh, or choose what will feed my soul?
2. What's something that I chase that leaves me empty?
3. What are some joyful "easter eggs" that God has placed that I often overlook?

REFLECTIONS:

DECLARATION TO GOD

God, I don't want to chase hollow things anymore.
I don't want to be fooled by what glitters but doesn't give life.
I want to run after what matters to You.
I choose fullness over flash.
I choose joy over empty thrills.
I choose You over the world's distractions.
Help me see the real treasure in front of me.
Help me not to miss the Easter eggs You've hidden all around me.
Today, I trade hollow for holy.

PRAYER

Father, I've wasted time chasing things that looked good but didn't last. Forgive me for the times I've let stuff distract me from Your goodness. Help me to turn my eyes back to You. Show me the beauty in the everyday moments. Show me how to live a full life—full of love, purpose, and You. Teach me not to trade what's eternal for what fades. Thank You for the joy You offer. I don't want a hollow life. I want a holy one. Amen.

GRATITUDE PROMPT

Write three godly treasures you're grateful for that make your life full:

____

____

____

____

____

Selah

Chapter 10

Quicksand of Delay

"If anyone, then, knows the good they ought to do and doesn't do it, it is sin for them."
James 4:17

Procrastination is a sly whisper, a tool the enemy wields with precision, and I've spent a lifetime mastering its art. It's the snooze button of the soul, a quiet promise that "later" will be better than "now."

Inside me, two wheels spin in constant battle. One churns with fire, eager to grow, expand, and evolve, pushing me to stretch into who I'm meant to be.

The other grinds low, begging to pause, to sit, to scroll through social media and let hours slip by. It murmurs, "First thing tomorrow, I'll tackle that thing," but tomorrow never comes.

It's quicksand thinking, soft, seductive, designed to keep you stuck.

Every morning, you wake up with a choice: sink deeper or step out. I've lingered too long in that muck, but I've learned this truth: the secret of life is action. It's getting up, moving, and choosing to push forward when the easy way is to stay still.

Life has to be met with small, actionable steps, even if they're not what you end up doing long-term. We have to master the art of moving, or we'll never break free; we stay stuck in quicksand.

After my last baby was born, I weighed a *small* 220 pounds. I think that's roughly the same as a baby hippo. It was a number that stared back at me from a scale like a mountain I didn't know how to climb.

Very morning, I'd wake up with the sun peeking through the blinds and tell myself, "Today's the day. Today I tackle my weight."

I'd picture eating right, walking, shedding the heaviness step by step. I only needed to take one small step at a time.

But then, as I lay there, the alarm buzzing, my hand would drift up and hit the snooze button. One tap, five minutes. Another small tap, ten more. It was so easy to push pause, to roll over and let the day slide by.

I'd tell myself, "I'll start after breakfast," then, "After lunch," then, "Tomorrow, first thing for sure." The bed was quicksand, and I sank into it day after day, trapped by the lie that delay was rest. That weight didn't budge—it grew heavier, not just on my body, but on my spirit.

The enemy loves that inertia. He whispers through procrastination, knowing it's a chain that binds us from God's call. Scripture cuts through the haze. James 3:17 says, *"If anyone, then, knows the good they ought to do and doesn't do it, it is a sin."*

Living a life with purpose is something we all know we should be doing. Therefore, by doing nothing with your life—as odd as it sounds—is a sin. It's robbing God of the thing He created you for.

I knew what I needed to do, but I kept hitting snooze. Satan doesn't need us to fall into wild rebellion. He just needs us to do nothing. To sit when we're called to rise. To scroll when we're meant to build.
But God? He's the God of *action.*

"Do not be afraid, do not be discouraged, for the Lord your God will be with you wherever you go" (Joshua 1:9). That's not a suggestion—it's a *charge* to *move*, to *step out of the quicksand* with Him on your side.

One morning, I'd had enough. The snooze button taunted me, but I swung my legs over the bed's edge instead. I stood, 220 pounds and all, and took a step—small, shaky, but *real.* I didn't have a grand plan, just laced up my shoes and walked out the door. It wasn't a marathon or even a diet overhaul.

It was a tiny move, a single push.

Day by day, I kept at it. Small, actionable steps—a walk here, a healthier meal there. They weren't always perfect, and some days I adjusted course, but I was moving.

The weight started to lift, but more than that, my soul did. Proverbs 13:4 became my anthem: "*The sluggard craves and gets nothing, but the desires of the diligent are fully satisfied.*" Action broke the chains procrastination forged. I wasn't stuck anymore.

Mastering the art of moving, even in small ways, will *set you free.*

Taking small steps can set big changes in motion, much like a push starts a snowball rolling downhill. In physics, Newton's law tells us that an object at rest stays at rest unless acted upon.

A concept proven in a 2015 study from *Physical Review,* where researchers showed even a tiny force can start a chain reaction in a static system, building *unstoppable momentum.*

Likewise, when you take a small step—writing one sentence or walking five minutes—you kickstart progress. Each move makes the next one easier, turning small efforts into a powerful force for transformation.

What did that look like in real life? For me, it started with one of my most over-the-top ideas ever...

The longest Slip 'N Slide in the world.

When the kids were little, I got it in my head to build the largest slip-and-slide in the world. Not just a long one. Not "Wow, cool backyard setup" long.

I mean record-breaking, Guinness-calling, epic YouTube fail compilation long. The kind of long that ends in a splash zone in another ZIP code.

Specifically? The reservoir behind our house. This was not a well-thought-out decision. This was a "woke up with a Bible verse and too much caffeine" kind of decision.

That morning, I had read: ***"Whoever watches the wind will not plant; whoever looks at the clouds will not reap."*** (Ecclesiastes 11:4)

And I took it personally.

"Enough waiting," I said to no one in particular, coffee in hand and toddler Velcro'd to my leg. "Today, we plant. With plastic."

I'm not one for half-measures when inspiration strikes, and this idea was pure genius. Or so I *thought.* Action's my new thing. I don't sit around pondering anymore.

So I piled the kids into the SUV—shoeless, cereal-stained, vaguely aware that something strange was happening—and drove to Home Depot like I was storming the beaches of Normandy.

I spent half our monthly food budget (yes, half—greatness comes at a price) on:

- 12 industrial-length garden hoses
- 3 rolls of Visqueen plastic, the size of baby whales
- 4 rolls of duct tape
- A pack of steaks for my post-slide victory meal

Did I have a plan? Absolutely not.
Did I know how long it needed to be? Not a clue.
Did I know how to connect hoses or avoid spinal injury?
That would be a no.

But I did have movement and a flamingo donut inner tube. I was moving, and that's what counts—taking a step, any step, even into the unknown.

We spent the whole day rigging it up.

Hoses duct-taped into a wiggly line that made no logical sense.
Plastic flapping like a blue tongue down the hill.

Stakes poked into the earth at reckless intervals. The backyard turned into a muddy bog, the children screamed with delight, and the dog got soaked and rolled in something dead.

I was alive. I was a mother on a mission. I was... in motion.

I didn't concern myself with angles or physics—I just did it, fueled by sheer will and a desire to do something with my day.

It was beautiful. Uneven. Wrinkled. A little cursed.

But *beautiful.*

"This is it," I told the kids, arms outstretched. "The longest slip-and-slide in the world. And we are sliding... into the reservoir."

They screamed. The dog barked. A neighbor stared from their window in alarm.

Did I measure anything? Nope.
Check the slope? No time.
Consider the large gravel patch halfway down the hill?
Oh, how *I wish* I had.

And then—Eric came home.

He got out of the car, briefcase in one hand, and just... stopped.

He looked at the muddy chaos. The flooded yard. The shrieking children. The very obvious liability issues unfolding before him.

He started spouting cruel words like "projection, trajectory, and structural integrity."

He adjusted his glasses. "Seriously, Melanie... what *is* this?" He said it all, professor know-it-all-like.

"The longest slip-and-slide in the world," I said proudly, hands on hips.
He stared. "There's a gravel patch in the middle."
"I know."

"You'll hit it going 30 miles an hour."

"It's fine."

"You've created a water-powered catapult."

I shrugged. "Momentum, Eric. Faith. Ecclesiastes. Planting season. You wouldn't get it."

He rubbed his face. "Okay, Melanie, then you go first. Before the kids."

Fair.

I climbed to the top of the hill with my pink inflatable flamingo donut, still inflated from last summer and now, possibly, a flotation device *and* a medical device.

I sat inside it like a queen on a rubber throne.

The kids chanted. "Mom, mom, mom, mom!" The sun was shining. The hoses gurgled to life.

"This is for glory!" I yelled. Giving my war cry, "This is for Ecclesiastes!"

"This is for MOM MOMENTUM!"

And then I *launched*.

And for one glorious second, I was a rocket. A legend. A human torpedo of inspiration and poor planning. My hair blew back. The wind howled. The flamingo screamed silently beneath me.

I was a *superhero!*

And then—

BAM.

Eric's big nerd words turned real. I hit the gravel patch like a sack of wet groceries. At a speed that clocked me into the record books, just not for the slip-and-slide.

My leggings disintegrated on impact—just exploded into static electricity and shame. I skidded down the hill, flamingo half-deflated, one side of my rear exposed to the neighborhood and the Lord Himself.

I came to a stop somewhere between "possible fracture" and "new tattoo made entirely of rocks."

Silence.

Then my youngest whispered, "Mom's butt is out."
Eric, still filming like David Attenborough narrating a wildlife disaster, said quietly, "Urgent care or full-blown ER?"

Take me to the emergency room.

I lay there, water misting into my face like some sort of baptismal regret, and I thought: This counts. This still counts.

Because momentum isn't always pretty.
It's not always clean.
Sometimes it's duct-taped, chaotic, and ends in gravel rash.

But it's still *forward.*

And Ecclesiastes was right. **If you're always waiting for the perfect conditions, you'll never plant.**

You'll never slide. You'll never feel the wind in your face as your flamingo donut lifts off for glory...

So yeah. Sometimes you'll crash.
Sometimes your leggings don't survive.
Sometimes your husband has video footage.

But you *moved.*

And that still matters.

Here's the kicker: Action doesn't always land you where you aim, but it's still forward motion. I learned that day—painfully—that projection and trajectory are not just big words. They're important things not to be ignored.

Setting a plan with purpose, then taking steps to make it happen.

Clearly, there's a balance in life between planning and acting. Some people map out everything but never move, stuck in fear or overthinking, while others move ahead with no direction, building slip-and-slides. Success comes from doing both—it's in the balance.

Don't wait for the weather to clear—to be perfect conditions.

Move *now*, even if it's just a shuffle.

Jonah, the prophet of the book of Jonah, embodies procrastination in a way that's almost painfully relatable. He knew exactly what God wanted, but kept putting it off with a mix of avoidance and excuses.

When God told him to head to Nineveh and warn its people to repent, Jonah didn't just delay packing his bags; he bolted for Tarshish, hopping a ship going the opposite direction. As if ignoring the task would make it disappear.

His reluctance wasn't mere laziness but a deeper resistance. He didn't want to face the Ninevites, or the possibility of their redemption, so he stalled, clinging to his own plans instead of God's.

This procrastination spiral only deepened until God intervened with a storm, a purge into the sea, and a three-day *time-out* in a fish's belly.

It took God's unrelenting push—vomiting him onto shore to finally drag Jonah out of his self-imposed delay and into the mission he'd been dodging.

His story reminds us that even if we're afraid, even if we can't see the vision realized, we have to start taking small steps toward it.

Because waiting for the perfect moment might just land you in deeper trouble.

You've got two wheels spinning, one to grow, one to stall. Choose the one that rolls forward, one small step at a time. It doesn't have to be the final answer, just a start.

I did: 220 pounds and a baby later, with a walk that turned into a *journey*, a giant slide that turned into a *life lesson.*

Get out of the quicksand, into life.

Get up. Move.

The victory's in the doing, and the path builds as you grow.

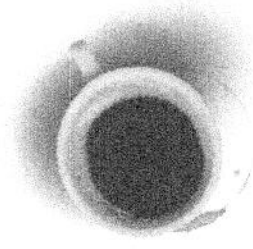

HEART CHECKS, DECLARATIONS & PRAYER

RETHINKING POINT:

Procrastination often looks like endless excuses—putting off tasks, scrolling instead of starting, or waiting for the perfect moment. It's hitting the snooze button on life. Small steps forward build momentum and purpose, even if you're scared to fail.

QUESTIONS TO ASK YOURSELF:

1. Do I take small steps toward my end goal, or do I hit the snooze button?
2. Am I afraid of failure, letting it keep me stuck in delay instead of disciplined action?
3. Am I walking in the direction that God is leading me?

REFLECTIONS:

God is Love

RETHINKING POINT:

Procrastination can disguise itself as busyness—filling your time without making meaningful progress. It's avoiding the hard stuff because failure looms, but taking intentional steps aligns you with where you're meant to go.

QUESTIONS TO ASK YOURSELF:

1. Am I clear on where God is leading me, or am I just keeping busy to feel productive?
2. Am I afraid of failure, choosing distractions over the direction I know I need to pursue?
3. What's one thing I have been putting off?

REFLECTIONS:

RETHINKING POINT:

Procrastination often looks like paralysis—overthinking every move until you do nothing at all, especially when failure feels like a shadow. But faithfulness to your purpose means starting small and trusting the process over fearing the fall.

QUESTIONS TO ASK YOURSELF:

1. When fear whispers "wait", do I respond in faith or freeze in overthinking?
2. Am I afraid of failure, letting it stop me from being faithful to do what I'm called to do?
3. Do I pray for God's perfect will in my life?

REFLECTIONS:

DECLARATION TO GOD

God, I declare that I am a person of action, not delay. I refuse to sit in fear, doubt, or comfort.

With You as my strength, I take steps forward—big or small—toward the purpose You've placed in me. I will not be paralyzed by perfection or procrastination.

PRAYER

Lord, You know the times I've stalled.

You've seen me stuck, scared to fail, or simply too tired to move. But I don't want to live that way anymore. Teach me to trust You with my first step, not just the final plan. Give me courage over comfort. Let me move, even if I wobble.

Let me build, even if I start small. Thank you for nudging my heart, even when it wants to linger. Give me the boldness to act, courage to obey, and faith that every step... even a small one... matters. In Jesus' name, Amen.

GRATITUDE STATEMENT

Today, I'm grateful for second chances, small beginnings, and the momentum that comes when I choose to move. Thank You, God, for the nudge, the grace, and the sacred reminder that progress doesn't have to be perfect to be powerful.

Chapter 11

Your Life Blueprint, No Tools Required

"In their hearts, humans plan their course,
but the Lord establishes their steps."
Proverbs 16:9

Picture this: It's early morning, the kind where the coffee's still brewing, and you're squinting at the world like, "Okay, God, what's the plan today?" You've got a notebook in front of you and maybe a slightly chewed pen because life's not perfect.

You're wondering how to figure out this whole purpose thing—not the big shiny stuff like, "*I want to be TikTok famous*" or "*I want a big yacht.*" God's already rolling His eyes at that.

This is about something *real,* something *you were made for*—something that, when you slip it on, feels like a pair of old sneakers.

Deep down, you know you were made for something *more*.

God didn't knit you together in your mother's womb just to binge-watch TV (though, let's be honest, that's tempting some days). He made you for a purpose, and your true purpose will always be about honoring God.

You're not just some cosmic accident, floating in the void like a misplaced sock in the dryer. God Himself, the ultimate master Weaver, the great I am, was up there in heaven—blueprint in hand—thinking: OK,

I'm knitting this one together. Needs a dash of curiosity, a sprinkle of stubbornness.

Let's throw in a love for Dad jokes (Eric), because who doesn't need comic relief in eternity?

Before the world could even whisper your name, God was there intimately weaving the threads of your life with *divine intention.*

You are not crafted by chance;
you are crafted with a purpose,
a unique calling edged into your very soul.

From the first beat of your heart to the dreams that stir within you now, every detail was designed by the Creator who knows you completely and loves you eternally.

Yet, in our human journey, we also wander from this divine path, seeking fulfillment in places that promises much but delivers so little. Things that bring temporary joy.

A new achievement, a fleeting relationship, material pursuits, physical beauty, all of them may spark happiness for a season, but eventually they all fade, leaving an ache that earthly comfort can't soothe.

Why? Because true peace, the kind that anchors us, making us solid through storms, comes only when we align with the purpose God has prepared for us.

Dear Reader, you were created uniquely for something only you can do, a role that glorifies God and blesses others.

Perhaps a knack for encouragement or a talent for turning mishaps into miracles.

Whatever it is, it's yours and your alone, only you can fulfill it.

There is only *one you!*

Me? Lately, my purpose is changing, and that's going to happen in life.

God gives us seasons, and if we're listening to His nudging, each season brings fulfillment.

In my new season, I think I'm supposed to create a space—nothing fancy, not some cathedral with stained-glass windows—just a little corner of the world where people who feel beat up by life can plop down, hear a story, and remember that God loves them.

I don't think I need to have this new season figured out; I just need to draw a sketch, and He will sharpen the lines.

One of my favorite stories in the Bible—in fact, it's the story that started me writing this book four years ago—is the story of Elijah.

Elijah stood weary on Mount Horeb, his spirit battered from battles, longing for direction. Depressed and wanting to die, he cried out, "What now, Lord?"

God answered, "*Go out and stand on the mountain before me*" (1 Kings 19:11). So Elijah stepped to the edge, his cloak whipping in the wind.

First came a mighty gust, so fierce it shattered rocks, but the Lord wasn't in the wind. Then an earthquake rumbled, shaking the ground beneath his feet—yet God wasn't in the quake.

Fire followed, roaring across the slope, a dazzling display of power, but God wasn't in the flame either. Elijah watched, for he knew God wielded the wonders. He'd seen it before.

Then, after the chaos faded, a gentle whisper brushed his ear—a still, small voice (1 Kings 19:12). Elijah pulled his cloak over his face, heart pounding, because this was different.

This was God drawing near, not in the thunderbolt, but in the quiet intimacy of a friend.

He is the Creator who is in the thunder—our miracles in life.
He is the God that is in our refining fire as well, but where does He long to meet us? *In the whisper.*

Think about it—you don't shout secrets to a stranger across a room. You lean in, voice low, to your closest friend, the one you trust with your heart.

That's a whisper, and that's what God craves with us—a bond so deep He can whisper, like a best friend sharing what matters most.

Why is it so important to listen to the whisper of God? Because it's in the gentle whisper in the day-to-day that the Creator can show you the purpose for your life.

But so often we don't see our purpose because we're not spending time waiting and listening for God's voice.

We somehow think God is so busy with the big things that He doesn't have time for a little, but in fact, that couldn't be more wrong!

My daughter, Kylie, used to drag me to this little fountain in our neighborhood every chance she got. It wasn't some grand, ancient relic —just a concrete circle with a trickling spout, surrounded by chipped chairs and the occasional pigeon strutting like he owned the place.

But to Kylie? That fountain was magic! She'd twirl around it, arms flung wide, sneakers scuffing—always on the edge of disaster.

She would dance like no one was watching, then—every single time—hit me with big, pleading eyes. "*Mom, can I have a coin? PLEEEASE? I gotta make a wish!*" Again and again, she would ask. Did I ever get mad or feel overwhelmed by her ask?
Nope, not once.

In fact, I would feverishly fish around the bottom of my purse—mostly finding lint, sometimes a crumpled receipt—but I would always find a penny or a dime just for her. Why?

Because the second the coin hit the water with a little plop, she'd squeeze her eyes shut, clasp her hands, and whisper her wish like it was the most important secret in the world.

"I wish for a puppy!" she'd say.
"I wish I could fly!" I never cared if her wishes were wild or downright impossible—
I just loved to hear her heart spill out.

Then one day, it hit me while she was spinning and wishing for a unicorn or whatever—
This is how God is with us.

Think about this. I would give Kylie that coin, knowing full well I wasn't going to be able to grant every wish. I couldn't sprout wings or keep a dolphin in our pool (which would have been bad for her—and the dolphin).

But I never stopped her from asking. I loved the ask. I didn't need to grant every wish for Kylie to know that I love her.

She'd dance, she'd wish, and then she would skip off, happy.

And God? He doesn't need to say yes to every prayer for us to know He's crazy about us.

Matthew 7:11 hits it home: "*If you then, though you are evil, know how to give good gifts to your children, how much more will your Father in heaven give good gifts to those who ask Him?*"

God wants to be in our everyday, in our every wish—even with ridiculous ones. He loves it when we trust Him.

He's never sitting there annoyed, like, "*Argh, another one from this guy!*"

No!

He's leaning in and smiling because every time we talk to Him—every dream, every hope, every goofy request—it's a step closer to Him.

It's a gentle whisper in the cave, talking to a friend.

And this is where our blueprint starts taking shape—it's building a relationship where God can freely talk to you and direct your steps.

Think of it like tuning a radio: life's noise, our worries, plans, and distractions all jam the signal. But when we turn down the volume and sit in silence, we can hear God's voice, clear and steady.

That voice isn't bossy or loud: it's gentle, like a friend pointing the way.

The bible in Psalm 46:10 says, *"Be still, and know that I am God."*

The stillness isn't just rest;
it's where we meet Him—
where He starts to show us our blueprint.

Prayer is how we talk to God about what our life will look like.

It's not a list of demands:
It's a *conversation.*

We ask, "What do you have for me?"

Then we *wait,* listening for His answer.

Sometimes it comes with a feeling, a nudge toward something we love, like helping people, creating things, or sharing ideas.

Other times, it's a quiet thought we keep coming back to.

But to hear, you have to hush the noise, turn off the TV, step away from the crowd, and let silence settle in.

That's where the magic happens.

It's not always instant. Sometimes you pray and listen for days, even months, before it clicks.

And that's okay, *God's not in a hurry.*
What matters is showing up, being still, and trusting He'll speak.

Your blueprint might start small, or maybe it's over the top. Both are amazing, ask, you can't offend God. Then, free ourselves in the relationship, God can start to build what He's already established inside of you.

Finding your blueprint isn't about forcing it; it's about uncovering what's *already* there. It's a seed planted when you were being formed, just waiting to get watered to *grow.*

Life gets messy when we ignore that quiet voice and try to figure it out ourselves. But when we pray and listen, God lights the path.

So, take a moment today. Find a quiet spot. Talk to Him. Then wait.

Your blueprint is waiting in that stillness, ready to bloom.

Psalm 139:13 says that He formed you in your mother's womb, created your innermost being, and knew every detail before you took your first breath.

So, who better to show you the blueprint of your life than the Father who drew it up in the first place?

Spend time with the One who created you so you can hear His whispers.

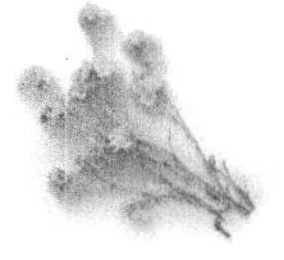

HEART CHECKS, DECLARATIONS & PRAYER

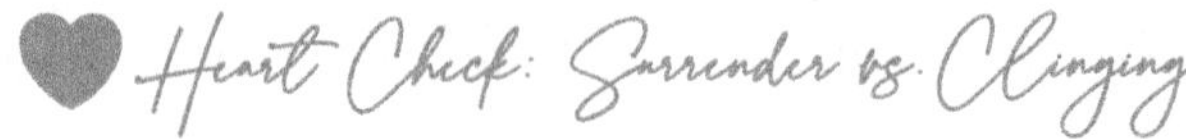

RETHINKING POINT:

God longs to speak in the quiet corners of your life, but that requires giving Him everything—your plans, worries, and desires.

QUESTIONS TO ASK YOURSELF:

1. Am I truly handing over every piece of my life to God, or am I clutching onto things that drown out His still, small voice?
2. Do I allow God to draw my blueprint?
3. Do I believe God sees me?

REFLECTIONS:

God is Love

RETHINKING POINT:

God's voice often comes as a whisper, not a shout, and He wants to meet you in the calm. If your life is too loud with distractions or constant motion, you might miss the time He's wanting to reveal His purpose to you.

QUESTIONS TO ASK YOURSELF:

1. Am I filling my days with so much noise that I can't hear God, or am I carving out quiet moments to listen for His direction?
2. Do I pray about every decision and direction in my life?
3. Will I say yes to paths that God wants me to walk, even when I can't see the path?

REFLECTIONS:

Heart Check: Trust vs. Control

RETHINKING POINT:

Giving everything to God means trusting Him enough to slow down and wait, even when you would rather take charge. He's in the subtle, intimate details of your life, but you have to be still and present to discern His will over your *own* impulse.

QUESTIONS TO ASK YOURSELF:

1. Do I trust God enough to stop striving and get quiet?
2. Am I too busy trying to figure it all out to hear what He's whispering to me?
3. Do I trust even when His no's are for my benefit?

REFLECTIONS:

DECLARATION TO GOD

"Even in the waiting, God is working. I will not lose heart. I believe His timing is perfect and His plans are good. What feels delayed is not denied. I am held, seen, and loved in every moment."

PRAYER

Father, I admit that waiting is hard. Help me to trust You even when I can't see the full picture. Strengthen my heart to remain faithful, hopeful, and at peace in the process. Teach me to rest in Your promises, and help me let go of trying to control the outcome. Thank You that You're never late, and You're never absent. In Jesus' name, Amen.

GRATITUDE PROMPT

Can you think of a time when God showed up? Can you see His timing was perfect?

____

____

____

____

____

____

____

____

____

Selah

Emma Cox

14 years old

A Life in Purpose

"Being confident of this,
that He who began a good work in you
will carry it on to completion
until the day of Christ Jesus."
Philippians 1:6

Have you ever felt like there's a pull inside of you? Something deep down that's been there since you were a kid? Maybe it's a dream you used to doodle in the margins of your notebook, or a spark that lit up when you created something out of nothing.

That's not an *accident.*

That's God's fingerprint on your life—a seed He planted long before you even knew how to spell your name.

It's worth noting the difference between a blueprint and a purpose, though they're woven together in God's design.

A blueprint is the essence of who you are—your talents, your passions, the unique way you're wired. It's the foundation, the raw material God starts with.

Purpose, though, is what you're created for—the mission He shapes from that blueprint, the way He calls you to be used to bless the world.

Think of it like this: If your blueprint includes a love for words, your purpose might be to write stories that inspire or teach truth. In the quiet, God shows you the "who" and the "what" so you can step fully into the life He's planned.

Years ago, I worked with kids who had been sexually and physically abused—a job I'd trained for with textbooks and late-night study sessions. I'd gone to school for it, earned a degree, but no matter how much I knew, it never fit me right—like a coat too tight in the shoulders.

The weight of their pain pressed down, married with the fact I couldn't have kids of my own, and though I wanted to help, I felt out of place—like I was forcing myself into a role that didn't match my wiring.

I could listen, comfort, and plan interventions, but my heart was always somewhere else. Deep down, I knew God had made me for something else—a purpose that I hadn't found yet.

I used to think purpose was this big, mysterious thing I had to chase down—like a treasure map with clues I could never crack.

I would look at my life, work, routine, and wonder:
"Is this it? Is this all I was created to be? Am I missing something, God?"

While waiting for a big moment, the big *aha* moment you're supposed to get—that defines the direction your life is going to take... I started doing something simple.

I started talking to God every day. Not long, elaborate prayers—just honest conversations. "Lord, show me what you see. What's the plan You have for me?" And I didn't just leave it there. I grabbed a notebook —a cheap one with a bent cover—and I wrote it down. Every nudge, every whisper I felt in quiet moments, I put on paper.

Here's the thing: *God doesn't leave us guessing.*

Proverbs 3:5-6 says, *"Trust in the Lord and cling to Him, and He will make our path straight."* That doesn't mean it's all crystal clear overnight.

It's more like a flashlight in the dark, showing you just enough for the next step. But the more you talk to Him, the more you see it—a blueprint that unfolds, piece by piece, guiding us to the purpose we were created for.

When David declared God's word is a lamp to his feet, he wasn't picturing a floodlight. In his time, a lamp was a small clay vessel, holding just enough oil to give off a soft glow. It didn't illuminate an entire field or brighten up a whole room. It gave only enough light for the next step.

God doesn't promise to show off the whole journey at once. He rarely reveals 10 steps down the road. Instead, He gives us the light we need for the moment we're in. His word guides us one decision, one act of obedience, **one step of faith at a time...**

Why does God work this way? Because trust grows us in the dark places between steps. If He revealed everything ahead of time, we would rely on our own sight, not His leading.

When the future is hidden, we must lean on His promises. When the path is uncertain, we discover the unshakable certainty of His character.

If we want to know our true purpose, we must be willing to close our eyes and hold God's hand and walk where He is leading us.

So how will we know our purpose?

Your purpose ties to what you're good at and what you love. God doesn't waste talents; He plants them in you for a reason. Maybe you're a natural storyteller, or you light up when you solve a problem. Pray into that. Ask God to show you how it fits into *His* plan.

What was my purpose? You know what I always keep coming back to? This little thing from when I was a kid. I loved creating things out of nothing—building skyscrapers out of sticks, choosing Lincoln Logs instead of Barbies.

I had forgotten that part of me, buried under doubt and distraction, but God hadn't. It's like He tucked that gift inside of me from the start, waiting for me to notice again. God didn't craft us just to appease our own dreams—He wove a purpose into our bones that stretches beyond us, touching others with His light.

Ephesians 2:10 says, "*For we are God's handiwork, created in Christ Jesus to do good works, which God prepared in advance for us to do.*" Like a lemon tree, we're made to bear fruit—but not in isolation or in the wrong place.

A lemon tree in Alaska's icy grip won't thrive—too cold, too harsh—no fruit will come where it does not belong. The tree might cling to life, its roots shivering in frozen ground, but it won't thrive.

It needs warm soil, careful tending, water, and sun to yield its tangy gift. So it is with us—if we don't live in the purpose God designed, rooted in His will, we'll never bear the fruit He intends.

We humans can endure tough environments, gritting our teeth through the cold, dark seasons of life, but survival isn't the same as flourishing. When we're stuck in a place that doesn't nurture our potential, we may persist, but we'll never fully blossom into the beauty or purpose we're capable of.

Just like that lemon tree, we're left stunted, always battling to survive rather than thriving in the warmth we were designed for.

Jesus once saw a fig tree by the road, full of leaves but barren of fruit (Matthew 21:18-19). Hungry, He cursed it, and it withered. Why? Because it wasn't fulfilling its purpose.

It looked alive but served no one—not even the One who made it. The same can be said for us—if we are just a tree with leaves, we're *alive but fruitless.*

But when we're planted in the right soil—God's Word, His Spirit, His calling for our lives—we don't just survive; we thrive, producing love, kindness, and hope for others. A lemon tree in rich earth feeds a family; a life in God's purpose feeds the world. Stray from that soil, and we're just leaves with no fruit—pretty but empty, standing but ultimately worthless. God sees us as orchards, not ornaments, and when we sink our roots into Him, we bloom for His glory.

My youngest daughter, Emme, at 15, is nothing short of amazing—a quiet force with a gift that leaps far beyond what you would expect from a teenager.

With just a pencil, she can sketch almost anything—a windswept tree, a friend's face, birds mid-flight—each line so precise it feels alive. She'll spend hours lost in the details—the feathers' texture, the shadows' depth —pouring herself into every stroke until it's perfect.

Time isn't relevant, sketching pictures, hours scamper off like playful pixies, and she gets so lost in time, convinced it's been only minutes, yet hours, even days have passed.

Her spirit's high, heart humming because she's drawing the lines she was meant to draw. With every swirl of her pencil, breathing life onto paper, she's content because she's in God's purpose.

When she hands someone her work, their eyes widen with joy. I've seen her sketches pinned in special places, even some framed on walls as art. I believe this is what God created her to do. It's not just a skill—it's a passion that fuels her, a fire she tends daily. A soil so warm and nurturing, it's easy for her to root.

She dreams of art school, of following where God leads, and I know her purpose isn't just for her. Her art blesses those around her, lifting spirits with every picture she creates.

Your purpose isn't meant to be a solitary treasure, locked away for your own fulfillment; it's a gift that ripples outward. Emme's purpose doesn't stop at her canvas.

She'll sit with others, patiently teaching them to sketch, guiding their hands to find their lines. Helping her brother with a project, a quiet suggestion, or taking the project over altogether.

When Rett's teacher asked him to draw a Mission from 1880. Rett just stared at the paper, because for him, anything past stick figures was medieval torture. How nice to have a sister who actually enjoys it.

Not everyone's built for the same assignments, and that's what makes us each so special. And why it's so important that we live for the purpose *we* were created for.

This is the true purpose: a servitude to God that flows naturally through gifts that brighten people's day. It's proving that living in God's design isn't selfish but a radiant act of love that transforms everything it touches.

Look at Bezalel in Exodus 31:2-5—God filled him with His Spirit and skill to craft the Tabernacle's beauty, from gold filigree to carved wood. His creativity was an act of servitude. Inspiring and leading His people to worship.

Emme's pencil is her tool; it fulfills her purpose. It's like me when I design a house, Will arriving on scene, Kylie in a plane, Sean building a house, Rett in God's house. Each person is unique, beautiful, and created for a purpose. God has created us not only for ourselves but for everyone in His kingdom.

Purpose not only fulfills us—it's bigger than that. It touches hearts, spreads light, and brings God's design to bless us all.

A life that honors God.

You have to really let this sink in and know this absolute truth:

YOU ARE NOT AN ACCIDENT!

God knew you from the start—exactly when and where you would be born, and to whom.

Scripture affirms this in Psalm 139:16, which says, "*Your eyes saw my unformed body; all the days ordained for me were written in Your book before one of them came to be.*"

Every detail of your existence was intentionally planned by a loving Creator, the author of life.

True fulfillment and a happy life come only when we step into the purpose God crafted for us. Anything less leaves us chasing shadows, mired in strife. It's a life in a ship without a rudder, tossed by every wave, but never arriving anywhere meaningful.

I've seen it happen, People hopping from job to job, marriage to marriage, church to church, always searching for something to fill the emptiness.

They're unfulfilled not because the world failed them, but because they haven't anchored themselves to a purpose that's bigger than their circumstances. Without clarity on why you're here, you'll spend your days reacting instead of pursuing, wandering instead of building.

Purpose isn't a luxury; it's a necessity.

It's a compass that keeps you steady when a storm hits—the lens that brings you into focus.

When you don't know what you're called to, every shiny opportunity looks like the answer. You switch careers because the paycheck doesn't satisfy you. You leave relationships because the spark fades. You abandon communities because they don't feel right anymore.

But the problem isn't the spouse, job, or pew—it's the lack of a north star guiding you.

Purpose won't end up as a vague feeling; it will be a concrete direction. A pastor once said, "Look at your gifts, your passion, the needs around you. Where those overlap, you will often find your calling. Once you know it, focus becomes your superpower."

A life of purpose has to have focus, not frenzy. You're not here to bounce from one fleeting passion to the next; you're here for a reason that's uniquely yours. Jeremiah 29:11 promises, *"For I know the plans I have for you,"* declares the Lord, *"plans to prosper you and not to harm you, plans to give you hope and a future."*

When we align with His design, life hums with meaning, and happiness is rooted in being who He made us to be.

Here's the truth: fulfillment doesn't come from finding the perfect job, partner, or community. It comes from knowing why you're in them. A man who knows he's called to teach will find joy in a classroom of rowdy kids, while another might quit in a month. A woman who knows she's meant to heal will endure the long nights of medical school, while someone else burns out.

Purpose turns the mundane into the meaningful. Without it, even the best things feel empty.

So stop drifting. Get quiet. Dig deep. Find what you're called into—not what's trending, but what's yours.

Then lock in.

The world is full of restless wanderers, switching lanes because they never pick a road. Don't be one of them.

A clear purpose isn't just a nice idea; it's the difference between a life lived well and a life that echoes behind you.

Choose focus. Choose clarity. Choose purpose.

And watch how everything falls into place.

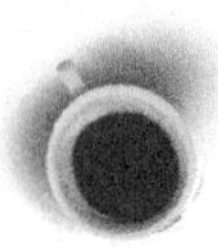

HEART CHECKS, DECLARATIONS & PRAYER

RETHINKING POINT:

Your purpose isn't just a personal perk; it's a platform to honor God and touch the lives of those He's placed in your path. Comfort might feel good, but it often pulls you away from the active, specific role God designed you for in His bigger story.

QUESTIONS TO ASK YOURSELF:

1. Am I okay with being passive and comfortable?
2. Am I pushing forward in my purpose to honor God and serve the people He's called me to impact?
3. Do I recognize that my purpose is a platform for His kingdom?

REFLECTIONS:

God is Love

Heart Check: Impact vs Ease

RETHINKING POINT:

God's plan for you includes a purpose that's bigger than your own life—a platform to reflect Him and bless others. Taking small steps toward where you're meant to end up means rejecting the lure of ease, knowing comfort can dull the specific kingdom role you're made for.

QUESTIONS TO ASK YOURSELF:

1. Am I choosing ease over the small steps that build a life honoring God?
2. Am I living boldly in my purpose as a platform for those I'm meant to reach?
3. Am I allowing God to fully direct my life?

REFLECTIONS:

DECLARATION TO GOD

- I declare that my life is not an accident. God has a plan for me.
- I declare that I am stepping into my purpose—one step at a time.
- I declare that the gifts God has given me are meant to be used for His glory and the good of others.
- I declare that I trust God's timing in my life, even when I can't see the whole picture.

PRAYER

Lord, thank You for the gifts and passions You've placed in me. Thank You for the blueprint You created in me, even before I was born. I pray that You would show me how to step boldly into the purpose You've designed for me. When I get discouraged or lost in the noise of the world, help me to focus on Your plan for my life. Give me the courage to take the small steps, even when I don't have the whole picture yet.

I surrender the plans I've made and the comfort I've settled into. Lord, let my life be a reflection of Your glory and a blessing to those around me. I trust that You're guiding me every step of the way. Amen

GRATITUDE PROMPT

What am I grateful for today? Consider the blessings, both big and small, that God has placed in your life.

____

____

____

____

____

____

____

The Great Vietnam—Cambodia Chaos: Positive Words at Work

"A cheerful heart is good medicine, but a crushed spirit dries up the bones."
Proverbs 17:22

If you've ever wondered what it's like to completely mess up an international trip, let me tell you.

And trust me, I can tell you.

It all started with a single oversight.

You know how, when you leave one country, you sometimes need a visa to get back into another? Well… I kind of forgot about that. Minor detail, right?

Where was I when this tiny-but-life-altering mistake came to light?

Oh, just having the absolute time of my life in Cambodia. Spa day with my daughters. Feet up, robe on—not a care in the world. Blissfully unaware that half my family was about to be catapulted into a full-blown international travel *nightmare.*

Picture this: I'm lying on a heated massage table, wrapped in a cloud of jasmine and eucalyptus. Soft music playing, gentle hands working tension out of my lower back with warm stones. I think I may have ascended to another dimension—somewhere between *nirvana* and a luxury-hotel commercial.

Meanwhile, back in Vietnam, the other half of our family—my husband, my son, and my daughter—were having a very different experience.

They had just landed after a short flight, expecting to breeze through immigration and reunite with us later that evening. Instead, they were pulled aside, asked a few too many questions, and then hit with the news: they couldn't re-enter the country.

No visa. No exceptions.

Apparently, when we all left for Cambodia, they assumed—I assumed—that we'd be allowed right back into Vietnam.

Turns out, that's not how it works. When you leave, you are required to apply for a new one for re-entry.

Oops.

So there they were, stranded in the airport, no hotel, no exit, no way to reach us right away.

Immigration officials calmly (and not very helpfully) informed them that their only option was to remain in the international terminal for the next thirty-six hours until the next flight back to the U.S.

And yes, that flight would take twenty-two hours once they made it on the plane—with a layover. *Of course.* Giving them something to look forward to.

Meanwhile, I'm sipping a ginger tea in a silk robe, wondering whether to go for the collagen facial or the full-body scrub next.

I didn't even look at my phone for hours. I was in spa mode—phones on silent. I emerge refreshed, floating on a cloud of lavender oil.

And when I emerged, I found 47 missed messages.

Three missed calls from Vietnam, immigration, and one very panicked voicemail from my husband.

I can't even describe the emotional whiplash.

I went from *"Namaste"* to *"Oh crap!"* in 0.3 seconds.

Needless to say, the rest of my spa day was canceled.

My daughters were still in their fluffy slippers when I started googling *"emergency Vietnam Visa,"* calling the consulate, and trying to get someone—anyone—to pick up the phone on a Sunday.

And the worst part? There was nothing we could do.
No last-minute Hail Mary.
No diplomatic miracle.

They had to wait it out. Sleep on the airport benches. Live off vending machine snacks. And then take a long flight home.

Jet-lagged, exhausted, and definitely not glowing from a facial.

So yeah, it all started with one tiny oversight.

Now, let's rewind a little.

We'd just finished our magical, picturesque days in Cambodia—sipping coconut water, basking in the sunset, walking through ancient temples. It was basically a Pinterest board come to life, and life was good.

Everything had gone perfectly—until they crossed over to Vietnam. I mean, who could mess up such an easy, fun, one-night trip, right? Well... me.

I could, and I did.
And I did it in *spectacular* fashion.

Let's add this little fact.

Today was Kylie's 20th birthday.

You can imagine how this could've turned them into whiny wet blankets—sobbing about missing the city and spending the night curled up on hard airport chairs—but nope!

They had been training their brains in positivity, and let me tell you, it paid off.

They'd learned the fine art of seeing the *good* in everything—a glass-half-full group.

I don't think I would have fared so well, but they're better at it than I am.

They found a dim, forgotten corner of the airport—think flickering lights and the distinct whiff of mystery meat—and they transformed it into their own five-star campsite.

Bags stacked like a fortress, makeshift blankets flung over chairs, and the world's most *questionable* floor mats as their carpet.

Instead of doom-scrolling their misery, they did the only logical thing: they *embarked on an adventure.*

A food-stall scavenger hunt.

Forget that the food could have been anything from frog legs to what might have been puppy pops—if it was edible, it was epic. They ate like culinary daredevils, grinning through each bite as if they were the stars of their own *foodie survival show.*

Think Anthony Bourdain, but without quality control.
Or "What's the weirdest thing I can eat today?"

Answer: *everything!*

They washed it all down with a cold Coke and a shot of *"We're here for the adventure!"* They moved on to Pokémon. I'm talking full-blown Pokémon Go mania, folks.

They were so deep into the game, Kylie got a "gym badge" notification on her 20th birthday. *"Take that, world! Beat you at your own game, even though I'm stuck in an airport!"*

But the real magic happened when they hit the shops like birthday pirates on a mission.
They didn't just buy gifts; *they ransacked the place.*

Plastic Buddhas—even though they weren't allowed it—and they bought keychains that read *"I Love Ho Chi Minh"* (seriously, who buys these things?), and other random trinkets no one knew existed.

Kylie's haul was an absolute mess—but one she proudly paraded as memories of her epic birthday.

Meanwhile, I was still back in Cambodia, blissfully unaware of the chaos.

Here I was, getting foot massages, sipping herbal tea, and enjoying the slow-paced life. *Totally* unaware that the people I loved the most were becoming pioneers of positivity in an airport hellscape.

They were sending me texts like *"Having the best time ever!"* and *"Kylie's birthday is unforgettable, Mom!"*

And all I could think was, *Wait, was I missing out?"*

They played card games, creating a tournament-style championship right there in the middle of the airport. Of course, they had to make up their own rules—like *you have to make up an accent for every card you play*—which led to them shouting at each other in ridiculous foreign accents and bursting into laughter.

What could've been a soul-crushing 36 hours of birthday blues turned into a legendary vacation finale. **They didn't just survive—they *thrived.***

They had a blast turning every inconvenience into an opportunity for fun. What was supposed to be a nightmare became a ridiculous, quirky, hilarious memory.

They proved that positivity isn't just a vibe—it's a *superpower.* They didn't just make the best of a bad situation—they straight-up *transformed* it.

What happened in that airport wasn't just a quirky travel story—it was a spiritual victory. You see, joy doesn't always come naturally. It's a decision.

An act of defiance in the face of disappointment. And biblically speaking, it's a form of *warfare.*

Scripture tells us that the enemy comes *"to steal, kill, and destroy"* (John 10:10). And often, he starts not by wrecking your circumstances, but by setting up camp in your mind—sliding into your thoughts, whispering lies, planting fear, feeding frustration.

He wants to convince you that the situation *is* hopeless. That you've been forgotten. That God has walked away. But the truth is, even in the middle of your delay, discomfort, or disaster, God has *already prepared a table for you* (Psalm 23:5).

A place of peace.
A feast of presence.

And the enemy has *no right* to sit there—unless you give him one.

When you choose negativity, anxiety, or resentment, it's like pulling out a chair for the accuser.

But when you choose gratitude—when you choose joy—even while stuck in a fluorescent-lit airport with mystery meat and lost plans? That's when you guard your table.

That's when you say,
"Not today, Satan."

Proverbs 17:22 says, *"A cheerful heart is good medicine."* That's not just poetic—it's powerful. Choosing joy isn't denial; it's dominion. It's refusing to let the enemy claim a victory in your mind.

And when you take your seat at the Lord's table, no matter what chaos is swirling around you, you feast on truth. You drink deeply of peace. You remember who sets the table—and who does not.

The enemy would've loved for my family to sulk and spiral on Kylie's birthday. He would've loved to see bitterness take root. But instead, they worshiped with laughter. They praised with silliness. They reclaimed joy in a place designed for waiting and discomfort.

It wasn't just a funny story. It was a spiritual declaration:
"We will not allow the enemy to set up camp."

Looking back, I realize it could've all gone so differently. That day could've been a disaster. But it wasn't—because they made a decision.

They chose joy.

And that's not always easy, is it? Choosing positivity doesn't mean ignoring reality. It means looking at the same situation with different eyes. It means refusing to hand over your peace to your circumstances.

Positivity is a conscious choice—a spiritual discipline, even. And when we practice it, something shifts—not just in us, but around us.

Because here's the truth: when we're negative, we shift the energy of every room we enter. We carry that heaviness like smoke, and others breathe it in.

But when we carry joy—even fragile, shaky joy—it multiplies. It lifts. It heals. It lights up dark corners—even airport corners that smell like mystery meat.

The enemy doesn't need an invitation—he just needs access.

A little crack of self-pity. A little whisper of bitterness. And then he's in—narrating your whole day. But you get to decide who sits at your table. And my family chose to fill theirs with laughter, scavenger hunts, weird food, and Pokémon.

As Psalm 23 says, "*You prepare a table before me in the presence of my enemies...*" That means you can feast—right in the middle of the battlefield. You can smile in the storm. You can sing in prison. You can play cards in the airport.

So, the next time life feels like a locked-down airport with flickering lights and the wrong snacks—don't panic.

Don't spiral. Don't hand the mic to the enemy.

Take the mic back. Reclaim your joy.

Transform the chaos into a campfire story.

You don't have to fake it. You just have to refuse to *fold.*

And that, my friend, is how a forgotten visa turned into the best worst birthday we'll never forget.

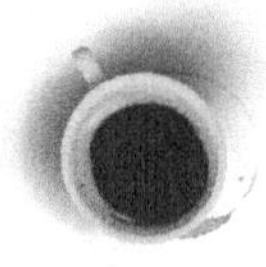

HEART CHECKS, DECLARATIONS & PRAYER

RETHINKING POINT:

Joy isn't circumstantial—it's spiritual. What if inconvenience isn't the enemy, but an invitation? Joy doesn't wait for everything to go right—it shows up when we choose it anyway. You don't need perfect conditions to create lasting memories. Sometimes, the messy moments—like airport scavenger hunts and mystery-meat dinners—become the stories we tell forever. What feels like failure—a forgotten visa or missed flight—could actually be a setup for breakthrough, bonding, and spiritual resilience.

QUESTIONS TO ASK YOURSELF:

1. Am I giving the mic to God's truth today, or letting the enemy's lies shape my mood?
2. Is my joy rooted in unshakable faith, or dependent on how comfortable life feels?
3. Have I been shifting the atmosphere with joy—or letting negativity shift me?

REFLECTIONS:

____

____

____

____

____

God is Love

Heart Check: Delay or Divine Setup?

RETHINKING POINT:

Delays don't always mean detours—they might be divine setups. What feels like a mistake or misstep may actually be the stage for growth, deeper trust, and unexpected miracles.

God's not just present in the plan; He's present in the pivot.

QUESTIONS TO ASK YOURSELF:

1. Am I letting joy be stolen by things that don't deserve that kind of power?
2. In the middle of inconvenience or disappointment, what am I handing over to the enemy without realizing it?
3. When things go wrong, do I default to self-pity—or choose to shift my perspective?
4. Am I carrying joy into the room—or waiting for the room to give it to me?
5. What spiritual muscle am I flexing in frustration?

REFLECTIONS:

____

____

____

____

____

RETHINKING POINT:

Joy is not a reaction—it's a rebellion. It doesn't ignore pain; it stands in the middle of it and says, "*You don't get the final word.*" When you choose joy, you're not just surviving—you're pushing back darkness with laughter, light, and faith.

QUESTIONS TO ASK YOURSELF:

1. Am I more focused on what went wrong—or what God might be doing in the middle of it?
2. Where is my attention: the chaos around me or the Creator within me?
3. What tone am I setting in hard moments—for myself and those around me
4. Am I radiating peace and playfulness, or inviting in panic and pessimism?
5. Have I made space for God at my table—or am I feeding frustration instead?
6. Who or what is getting fed by my thoughts, my words, and my energy today?

REFLECTIONS:

____

____

____

____

____

____

BONUS ROUND:

Your mind is a garden, and your thoughts are the seeds.

Twelve minutes of intentional, positive prayer each day for eight weeks can reshape your brain's neural pathways toward peace and resilience.
Toxic thoughts, fear, and unforgiveness act like weeds, disrupting mental clarity and releasing stress hormones like cortisol, which can damage both brain and body over time.

Choose to plant thoughts of gratitude, love, and trust to cultivate a healthier mind and life.

BONUS ROUND QUESTIONS:

1. Pause and notice your thought patterns. Are you dwelling on fear or unforgiveness, which can tighten your chest or raise your pulse? Shift to a prayer of gratitude for one thing in your life.
2. Am I holding onto poison? Unforgiveness and anxiety are like toxins. Ask yourself—what grudge or worry am I holding onto? Offer it up in prayer, visualize it leaving your body, and open space for healing and renewed connections.
3. Where is my focus anchored? Your brain follows your attention. Am I replaying worst-case scenarios, or am I grounding myself in hope? Spend a moment praying for someone else. This redirects your mind to purpose and love. Always reinforce positive pathways.

DECLARATION TO GOD

God, I choose joy—not because everything is perfect, but because You are present. I refuse to let frustration, fear, or bitterness sit at my table. I make room for peace, laughter, and Your truth. Even when plans fall apart, I know You are still working for my good. Help me to see delays as invitations, inconveniences as opportunities, and each moment as sacred. You say you have prepared a table for us, even in the middle of our mess, Psalm 23:5 says. I can feast on your peace even in the presence of disappointment. Thank You for joy that defies logic. I will trust You in every airport of life.

PRAYER

Father, Thank You for meeting me even in unexpected places. When life stalls and plans fall through, help me find You in the middle of it. Teach me to laugh, to praise, and to hold onto joy. Remind me that the enemy cannot steal what I refuse to surrender. Whether I'm in a palace or a terminal, I choose to see Your goodness. You are the God who turns waiting into worship and chaos into connection. Amen.

GRATITUDE PROMPT

Write three things that brought you joy this week—especially things that didn't go according to plan:

1. ______________________________
____

2. ______________________________
____

3. ______________________________
____

Selah

through faith. And I pray that you, being rooted and established in love, 18 may have power, together with all the Lord's holy people, to grasp how wide and long and high and deep is the love of Christ, 19 and to know this love that surpasses knowledge—that you may be filled to the measure of all the fullness of God.

God is love. Whoever lives in love lives in God, and God in them. 17 This is how love is made complete among us so that we will have confidence on the day of judgment: In this world we are like Jesus. 18 There is no fear in love. But perfect love drives out fear,

Christ even when we were dead in transgressions—it is by grace you have been saved. 6 And God raised us up with Christ and seated us with him in the heavenly realms in Christ Jesus, 7 in order that in the coming ages he might show the incomparable riches of his grace, expressed in his kindness to us in Christ

37 No, in all these things we are more than conquerors through him who loved us. 38 For I am convinced that neither death nor life, neither angels nor demons, neither the present nor the future, nor any powers, 39 neither height nor depth, nor anything else in all creation, will be able to separate us

5 And hope does not put us to shame, because God's love has been poured out into our hearts through the Holy Spirit, who has been given to us. 6 You see, at just the right time, when we were still powerless, Christ died for

be done for you. 8 This is to my Father's glory, that you bear much fruit, showing yourselves to be my disciples. 9 "As the Father has loved me, so have I loved you. Now remain in my love. 10 If you keep my commands, you will remain in my love, just as I have kept my Father's

Pruned for Purpose

"If anyone, then, knows the good they ought to do and doesn't do it, it is sin for them."
James 4:17

Gardening has always been my sanctuary. I love being outdoors, digging into the soil, coaxing life from tiny seeds, and watching branches stretch toward the sun.

But even in a thriving garden, balance is everything. Sometimes, trees heavy with too much fruit or too many branches buckle under their own weight.

The fruit turns tasteless; the branches grow weak.

That's when pruning comes in. You have to cut back even the living branches so the rest can grow stronger—producing better, healthier fruit.

In John 15:1-2, Jesus says, *"I am the true vine, and my Father is the gardener. He cuts off every branch in me that bears no fruit, while every branch that does bear fruit, He prunes so it will be even more fruitful."*

God's care can seem direct—even harsh—but it's always purposeful: trimming us back to make us whole. This chapter is about balance—about how God's tests are pruning moments, not punishments.

And how our response to them shapes our growth.

I've learned from gardening that pruning isn't about destruction—it's about restoration and health. A branch might be alive—even bearing fruit—but if it's overburdening the tree, it has to go. Left unchecked, the whole plant suffers.

God works the same way in us. When He prunes, it's not to wound us anew but to expose old hurts—wounds we've buried and pain we've ignored. It's how we grow in integrity.

The process stings. It's a test of endurance.

Yet if we skip it—dodging the shears because we dread the cut—we only prolong the pain. A diseased branch left uncut spreads rot to the rest of the tree.

God doesn't prune to hurt us but to keep the sickness from taking over. He cuts to make us healthy—to help us bear sweeter fruit. But oh, how we hate tests! As children of God, we recoil at the word. It conjures images of failure—red marks on a page, or stumbling in front of a crowd.

When God tests us, we often see it negatively—especially when the trial drags on longer than we expect.

People get angry, frustrated. Some even walk away from Him because the weight feels unbearable.

So why do we despise tests? Because we fear they'll reveal our weakness—that we'll fall short. But God's goal isn't failure—it's flourishing.

It's not punishment. It's a promotion.

David understood this when he prayed, *"Test me, Lord, and try me; examine my heart and my mind."* He didn't shrink from the process—he saw it as a chance to grow closer to God.

What if we reframed tests as promotions? People hear "test" and brace for defeat, but God sees it differently.

When He prunes, He's preparing us for *more*—more strength, more fruit, more understanding, more life.

It's not a mark of shame but a vote of confidence.

Think of a gardener pruning a tree—not because it's failing, but because it's ready to thrive.

God tests us to refine us—to strip away what weighs us down and lift us higher. The process of pruning isn't comfortable.

When He cuts, it can feel like loss—a dream deferred, a relationship ended, a season of struggle. These are the shears at work. But He's not creating new wounds—He's tending to the old ones: branches we've let fester, hurts we've masked with busyness or denial.

Or maybe, just maybe, He's taking us into a wilderness to teach us, to grow us, to make us strong. So when we come out, we not only realize the provision of God but the POWER of God!

As much as you'll hate to hear this, **it's in the wilderness that God makes us unstoppable!**

So why does it feel like punishment?

I don't believe God smites us with punishment. He's not up there hurling lightning bolts. Our pruning is either for our good or from our own choosing.

Sometimes we're pruned not for our good but because of our free will. When we choose to drift from His ways, we leave the shelter of His peace, and the world creeps in.

I always imagined God's grace and protection like a vast, sheltering umbrella—its canopy woven from threads of divine love and mercy, arching protectively over us in the storms of our life.

When we rest beneath it, we are cradled in His grace and protection, safe from the world's downpours.

Yet the instant we choose to wander off—the second we choose to leave the umbrella—His heart aches with profound sorrow; our choices create a chasm that grieves Him deeply because even though it is His desire to protect us.

It's our free will that left the protection.

And we're going to get wet...

It's just the nature of how things go.

Then there was the "Toaster Test"—and why I ended up in the Target line twice...

It was December 23rd, the official Procrastinator's Olympics, and I was representing Team "Waited Too Long."

Target looked like a scene from one of those end-of-the-world movies—carts clashing like bumper cars, toddlers melting down in every aisle, and a symphony of holiday stress rising like fog.

It was festive in a Lord of the Flies kind of way.

I marched in, fueled by caffeine and desperation, ready to conquer. I needed presents for the kids, stocking stuffers, a roll of tape (which I'd forget anyway), and apparently, my soul—because I would later lose it in the parking lot.

After surviving what can only be described as a slow crawl of shared suffering through the checkout line, I finally made it out.

I had dolls. Trucks. A shiny red toaster for our kitchen that I honestly didn't remember putting in the cart—but I accepted it as divine intervention.

I trudged out into the parking lot—which, by the way, was so far from the store I briefly considered applying for a permit to camp overnight.

I was halfway to my car, bags hanging off my arms like ornaments on an exhausted Christmas tree, when I stopped.

Wait a second.

The cashier hadn't rung up the toaster.

I froze mid-step. It was still in the cart.

Unpaid. Untouched. Mine... but not really.

Now listen—I didn't steal it on purpose. I wasn't wearing a ski mask.

But this was one of those soul-whisper moments—when the Holy Spirit taps your shoulder and says, "Well?"

And my brain—bless it—instantly went into negotiation mode:
It's Target. They make billions. The line's too long. I'll pay for it later.

Jesus understands—it's almost His birthday.

But deep down, I knew this wasn't about a toaster.

This was about my heart.

God's tests aren't usually dramatic.

There's no booming voice or lightning bolt.

More often, it's just you, a shopping cart, and a choice.

That day, I chose wrong.

I compromised—not in some huge, scandalous way, but in that subtle moment where convenience outweighed conviction.

I got in my car, toaster still wedged in the trunk, and drove home feeling like I'd flunked a pop quiz I didn't know I was taking.

God doesn't send punishments like thunderclouds.

He's not petty like that.

But when we step outside His covering—when we wander off the narrow path—we make ourselves more vulnerable to the chaos waiting in the world.

That chaos came knocking fast. By morning, the back window of my car was smashed—shattered like my pride. Everything was gone.

The dolls. The trucks. Even the morally questionable toaster.

All of it.

I stood there in my robe and fuzzy socks, glass crunching underfoot, staring at the wreckage and whispering, *"Seriously?"*

But I knew I'd failed the test—not because God was mad at me, but because my own actions had opened the door. I'd stepped out from His protection. And the world—well, the world doesn't play nice.

On Christmas Eve, while other people were sipping cocoa and admiring twinkle lights, I was back at Target with the other regret-ridden zombies, back in the same line, back buying everything I'd lost.

My kids deserved a Christmas. But this time, the lesson burned.

God trims us with tests, pruning away what doesn't bear fruit. On December 23, He was pruning my procrastination, my willingness to bend the truth, and my stubborn self-reliance.

That dumb toaster became a symbol—of the ways I'd been cutting corners: spiritually, emotionally, even in how I valued small decisions.

God wasn't mad. He was pruning me.

Trimming off the parts of me that thought shortcuts were harmless. Clipping the overgrowth of procrastination, of rationalization—part of me that always thought, *I've got this on my own.*

Spoiler: I don't. The pruning hurts. It always does. But it left me lighter. Straighter. **Rooted deeper in truth.**

The *bigger picture...*

Every day, God gives us choices. Some are huge—career paths, relationships, forgiveness. But many are small. Ordinary. Mundane. A shopping cart. A toaster.

A whisper that says, "Do the right thing, even when no one's watching." I've learned that integrity isn't tested in stadiums. It's tested in parking lots.

We like to think obedience is for the big moments—when in truth, it's the small ones that build our character brick by brick... or crack it apart, one compromise at a time.

God's trimming isn't punishment. It's preparation. He cuts away the dead stuff so we can grow stronger. So the fruit we bear isn't rotten.

So when storms come—and they will come—we're not toppled by the weight of our own self-made mess.

Integrity is built in parking lots. Patience is formed at checkout lines. Grace is forged in your reactions, not your resolutions.

I used to think obedience was about the big stuff—crossroads moments and deep valleys. But now, I see it's in the everyday—the tiny whispers where God says, *Choose Me. Choose what's right, even if it costs you comfort.*

And the thing is—when you walk that road, even when it's hard, there's peace. There's protection. There's the quiet joy of knowing your heart stayed true.

So now, I pay for my toasters. I keep my receipts. And when I hear that still, small voice, I don't ignore it. Because I'd rather walk the long line of obedience than live with the smashed window of compromise. I've learned that a $29.99 mistake can turn into a thousand-dollar lesson if I'm not paying attention. And hey—if God can use a missing toaster to prune my soul—He can use anything. Even Target.

It's about trusting the Gardener's hand.

Jesus' words in John 15:1-2 remind us: pruning is an act of care. He doesn't cut carelessly. Every snip has purpose. Every test is a promise.

We might not see it in the moment—when the shears are sharp and the branch falls heavy—but God's vision is bigger than ours. He's not just tending a single season; He's shaping a lifetime of growth.

If we trust Him through the process, we'll find that what's left behind is healthier, more vibrant, more *us* than we ever imagined.

So when the tests come—and they *will*—don't run. Don't let the sting of the cut or the length of the trial push you from God.

See it as pruning—a promotion to something greater.

God prunes us not to break us, but to balance us. To heal what's hidden. To make us whole.

Gardening has taught me that pruning isn't about cutting away—it's about strengthening what remains.

Sometimes, even a healthy branch has to go if it's pulling the whole tree off balance.

Samson's story, found in Judges, shows us this. He was raw power—hands that tore lions apart, shoulders that toppled gates, a jawbone that became a weapon of mass destruction.

Born a Nazarite, set apart by God to deliver Israel from the Philistines, his purpose was written into his bones.

But for years, that purpose drowned in pride.

Samson's strength wasn't the problem. His swagger was. To become who he was meant to be, he had to prune away the arrogance that kept chasing glory for himself instead of God.

His story is a jagged lesson in how cutting away pride can turn a wreck into a redeemer.

Pride was Samson's shadow, trailing every step. He flaunted his might, picked fights, and toyed with danger—trusting his strength to bail him out.

Pride whispered that he was untouchable, that his gifts were his to wield however he pleased. He didn't need vows, caution, or counsel—just his own grit.

But that hubris led him straight to a barber's chair. His eyes were gouged out. He was grinding grain in a Philistine prison. Pride didn't just trip him—it chained him.

But the story doesn't end there.

Stripped of his hair, his sight, and his freedom, Samson faced a choice: wallow in the ruin or prune what got him there.

In that dark cell, something shifted. When the Philistines dragged him out to mock him, he didn't strut or rage.

He prayed: "*O Lord God, please remember me and strengthen me just this once.*"

No bravado. No bluster. Just a plea.

That was the cut—pruning the pride that had ruled him, humbling himself before the One who had called him.

In that moment, he wasn't the showoff anymore—he was the servant.

And that pruning unleashed his purpose. With his hands on the pillars, Samson didn't flex for the crowd—he pushed for Israel.

The temple crashed. The Philistines fell. He delivered more in death than in all his proud years combined.

Strength wasn't his legacy. *Pruning* was.

What's your pride? What needs pruning?

Samson was loud—trusting brawn over calling. Yours might be quieter. Maybe it's the need to prove yourself.

To always be right. To control the show.

It feels like it's holding you up. But it's a weed, choking what you're meant to become.

Samson didn't see it until he was blind. But you don't have to wait that long.

Pruning pride stings. It means admitting you're not the center—that your gifts aren't yours to flaunt.

Yet it's the only way to make room for your real strength.

Samson's life shouts it: **Purpose waits on the other side of what you're willing to cut.**

He had to lose everything to prune pride. But you can choose it.

Let it go—the strut, the self-reliance, the spotlight.
Whatever it is that's weighing you down.

The pruning won't leave you weak. It will reveal the *you* that you were meant to be.

Samson brought down a temple when he did.

What can you build?

Tests will come daily.

There are old grudges, unspoken fears, and habits we cling to like overgrown branches.

Unhealthy patterns we've normalized.

Every time God steps in to prune, it hurts.

I used to cry out, "Why now? Why this?"

But looking back, I see He was balancing me—trimming what was weighing down my spirit, exposing wounds I hadn't faced, so the rest of me could grow stronger.

Like a tree after a good pruning, I stood taller.

My fruit was sweeter. My roots: deeper.

It wasn't easy—but it was always necessary.

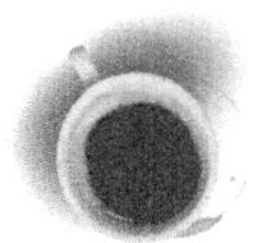

HEART CHECKS, DECLARATIONS & PRAYER

RETHINKING POINT:

- In gardening, pruning can look harsh. Cutting off even healthy branches feels extreme—until you realize it's the only way for the plant to thrive. God's pruning works the same way. He doesn't cut to punish. He cuts to heal. He trims back overgrowth—our pride, procrastination, and compromise—so we can become stronger, healthier, and more fruitful.
- Sometimes the smallest tests—a shopping cart decision, a whisper of conscience—reveal what still needs cutting.
- God doesn't trim us to make us smaller. He trims us so we can grow.

QUESTIONS TO ASK YOURSELF:

1. Do I allow God to prune things in my life that I know aren't good for me, or do I keep holding onto them?
2. Is there something rotten in my life I refuse to let go of, even though I know it's weighing me down?
3. Do I hold onto what's not good for me—even if it stunts my growth—or can I trust God to shape me into something strong and freer?

REFLECTIONS:

___

___

___

God is Love

RETHINKING POINT:

Sometimes there's a rotten piece—a habit, relationship, or mindset—you refuse to release, believing you can still salvage it. But God's refining fire isn't punishment; it's purification. Trusting Him means letting go so He can clear the decay and make room for new growth.

QUESTIONS TO ASK YOURSELF:

1. Is there something rotten in my life that I refuse to let go of?
2. Do I truly believe God's refining fire is taking things out for my good—or am I resisting because I don't trust His process?
3. Can I willingly let God trim back my overgrowth—pride, procrastination, compromise... to become healthier?

REFLECTIONS:

____

____

____

____

____

____

____

____

____

RETHINKING POINT:

When God removes things, it can feel like you're being burnt—left raw and exposed. But His fire purifies; it doesn't destroy. Seeing it as a process of becoming healthier rather than experiencing loss shows you trust that He's refining you for a greater purpose.

QUESTIONS TO ASK YOURSELF:

1. Do I see God's refining fire as being burnt, or as purifying me?
2. Do I believe He's removing things from my life to make me better —or do I hold onto what's harmful because I fear change?
3. Do I believe God doesn't prune me to make me small but to help me grow?

REFLECTIONS:

DECLARATION TO GOD

God, I trust Your shears.
Even when it stings, I know You are shaping me.
Help me let go of the things that weigh me down.
Prune what needs to go—habits, attitudes, pride, distractions.
Cut away the dead things so my life can flourish in You.
I choose growth over comfort.
I choose Your way over my convenience.
Make me fruitful in ways that honor You.

PRAYER

Father,
You are the Master Gardener. You know what needs to stay and what needs to go. Sometimes I resist the cut because I fear the loss—but today, I surrender. Prune my life so it bears the kind of fruit that lasts. Remove anything that stunts my growth. Teach me to trust Your process. Help me to see every test as an opportunity—not for punishment, but for promotion. Thank You for loving me enough to shape me. Even in the pain, I know You are good. Amen.

GRATITUDE PROMPT

Write three ways God has used hard seasons to help you grow:

1. ____
____

2. ____
____

3. ____
____

Selah

through faith. And I pray that
you, being rooted and
established in love, may have
power, together with all the
Lord's holy people, to grasp
how wid

God.

Amen.

Lamentations

But this I call to mind

and therefore

The steadfast love of the
Lord never ceases;

1 John 4
15 If anyone acknowledges
that Jesus is the Son of God,
God lives in them and they in
God. 16 And so we know and
rely on the love God has for
us.
God is love. Whoever lives in
love lives in God, and God in
them. 17 This is how love is
made complete among us so
that we will have confidence
on the day of judgment: In
this world we are like Jesus.
18 There is no fear in love. But
perfect love drives out fear.

Christ even when we were
dead in transgressions—it is
by grace you have been saved.
6 And God raised us up with

39 neither height nor depth, nor
anything else in all creation,
will be able to separate us

5 And hope does not put us to
shame, because God's love
has been poured out into our
hearts through the Holy Spirit,
who has been given to us.
6 You see, at just the right
time, when we were still
powerless, Christ died for the
ungodly. 7 Very rarely will
anyone die for a righteous
person, though for a good
person someone might
possibly dare to die. 8 But God
demonstrates his own love for
us in this: While we were still
sinners, Christ died for us.
9 Since we have now been
justified by his blood, how
much more shall we be saved
from God's wrath through
him! 10 For if, while we were

Shadow and Light

"Do not be anxious about anything, but in every situation, by prayer and petition, with thanksgiving, present your requests to God. And the peace of God, which transcends all understanding, will guard your hearts and your minds in Christ Jesus."
Philippians 4:6-7

Nights are always my worst. Fear has a way of stretching time, wrapping itself around your mind until you feel like you can't breath. I woke up often in the middle of the night, jolted from sleep by dreams I couldn't shake—visions of my children in danger, their futures crumbling, their lives unraveling.

Safety, marriages, happiness, friends—I feared for it all. A mom's quiet terror that never slept. Often in the midnight hours, I would slip out of bed, sneak across the floor across the house to whichever child had stirred me in that night's nightmare.

There I'd sit, hunched on my hands and knees—one arm outstretched like a lifeline, praying over them and whispering, desperate words:

"God, keep them safe. God guide them. God don't let them fall."

More often than not, they'd stir awake—three or four in the morning—eyes wide in fright at the sight of me, a shadowy figure hovering in their room. My vigil had a cost: eyes flying open, screams piercing the silence. To them, I wasn't a loving, praying mom—I was a shadowy figure looming in the dark, a stranger in their room.

"Mom, why?" they'd shriek, clutching their blankets, scared to death—certain they were caught in a home invasion.

Their little bodies would shake, thinking a burglar had crept in, ready to strike. I'd hush the guilt choking me, "It's just me, you go back to sleep. I'm so sorry—I didn't mean to wake you."

But the damage was done, my fears had sparked theirs. I should have learned some sort of lesson, yet I kept doing it—night after night,—year after year—crawling through the shadows, kneeling by their beds, frightening them half to death with my midnight prayers.

Even now, with them grown, there are nights I still wrestle that urge. Not that I don't know better—the kids have just learned to barricade their doors.

One fear I have, one child dug deeper than the rest, carving a trench in my soul. But God's story is always bigger than my fears.

When my son was little, the world of words didn't come easily to him. Dysphasia tangled his thoughts, twisting the pathways between what he felt and what he could say.

Speech became a mountain too steep to climb, and the pressure to scale it too much to bear. Stories—those beautiful bridges of connection—felt like puzzles missing half their pieces.

It didn't seem worth the struggle. So he stayed silent. His voice remained locked behind a wall I couldn't breach, no matter how gently I knocked.

The doctor told me not to worry—said it was something he'd likely outgrow, that his brain just needed time to sort itself out. I nodded politely, holding back the storm rising inside me.

But deep down, I didn't believe it. I knew this boy—his depth, his softness, his fierce inner world—I feared that the very things that made him beautiful would be buried beneath the noise of a world that didn't understand.

I'd watch him, this quiet boy—watcher of everything and speaker of so little. And I would wonder: *What words are spinning inside him that he can't—or won't—share?*

I tried to draw him out. I offered up playdates like lifelines, hoping another child might coax him into laughter, conversation, connection.

"Do you want a friend to come over today?" I'd ask. "Someone to play with?" But he'd just look at me with those steady, soulful eyes—the kind of eyes that seemed to see straight through the surface of things—and say, with quiet certainty,

"That's okay. You are my Bubbies."

I still remember the first time he said it. His voice was small, but the words were so sure. So complete. I felt the sting of tears immediately—because those words were a gift and a wound all at once. They were a balm and a blade—sweet in their trust, but heavy with the weight of solitude.

He wasn't choosing *alone* because he didn't want love. He just couldn't handle the demands of a world that required so much from him. Constant conversation felt like combat. Eye contact was a strain. Small talk—a foreign language.

So he retreated—not in bitterness, but in self-preservation. He found comfort in corners, solace in silence, safety in staying small.

He chose the company of me and Jesus.

There, in his quiet corners, I would find him. Sometimes curled up with a blanket, looking out the window. Sometimes just sitting in stillness.

And I would feel this ache I couldn't name—a mother's ache. The kind that lives deep in your chest and crawls up into your throat, but has no real name. A longing to fix something that might not be mine to mend.

I worried constantly—worried that I was missing something. That *he* was missing something. That his world would shrink so small he'd disappear into it.

And yet, even in the silence, I could sense something sacred happening —something I couldn't explain. While he wasn't talking to people, he was talking to God.

All those wordless hours, those seemingly empty moments—I believe now they were filled with quiet communion.

I'd mistaken it for isolation.

But while I saw a boy cut off from the world, Heaven saw a soul connected to eternity.

He was content.

And that contentment, oddly enough, frightened me.

It felt like I was losing him—like I was watching a ship drift slowly out to sea while I stood helplessly waving from the dock.

Come back, I wanted to shout.
You need friends. You need words. You need the world!

But what I didn't know—what fear blinded me from seeing—was that while I was desperate for him to speak to the world, he was already speaking with Heaven.

What looked like withdrawal was actually worship.
What seemed like retreat was a sacred relationship.
And what I called silence, God called sanctuary.

But fear doesn't see clearly. It clouds your vision. It exaggerates.

It distorts the truth until you can't tell the difference between protection and punishment.

Fear told me I was failing him.
Fear whispered that he was falling behind.
Fear hissed that he'd be lonely forever. *And I believed it.*

Night after night, I'd slip into his room once he was asleep. The soft hum of his white noise machine filled the air, and his peaceful little face would shine beneath the dim nightlight like a tiny moon.

I'd fall to my knees beside his bed and whisper the same prayers, night after night, through tears that wouldn't dry:

"God, make a way for him."
"Open doors he can walk through."
"Let him find his voice."

But under those prayers was a deeper cry I couldn't always admit. A cry that asked:

God, are You still good?
Can You be trusted with the child I love more than life itself?
Have You forgotten us?

I didn't lose sleep because of colic or teething. I lost sleep because fear had taken up residence in my heart. I'd lie awake, scrolling through worst-case scenarios in my mind. Diagnoses. Social delays. Future loneliness. The imagined weight of every silence became a prophecy I feared might come true.

That's the thing about fear—it's not just a feeling. It's a strategy.

The enemy doesn't always need to destroy you. He just needs to distract you long enough that you forget who God is.

Fear paralyzes. Fear distorts. And when we let fear speak louder than faith, we shrink God down to the size of our circumstances.

We stop believing His promises could apply to this—to us.
We stop trusting that He could actually turn this for good.

I see it now: how fear became a form of idolatry in my life.

I didn't bow to fear, but I sure listened to it. I gave it authority. I let it steal joy, peace, sleep, and presence—not because the struggle wasn't real, but because I stopped looking up.

But God.
In His mercy, He was already at work.
While I wept, He wove.
While I worried, He whispered.
While I watched and waited, He was watering seeds I didn't even know had been planted.

It didn't happen all at once. There wasn't a breakthrough moment with confetti and fireworks. It was slow. Sacred. Holy.

But one day, I heard him speak—
not just to me, but about Jesus.

He prayed with a depth that stunned me.

He quoted Scripture—not because he had memorized it from a workbook, but because he had held it in the silence.

Absorbed it.
Let it become part of him.

His faith hadn't just survived the silence.
It was *built* in it.

God had been moving all along.

Romans 8:28 came alive before my very eyes: *"And we know that in all things God works for the good of those who love Him, who have been called according to His purpose."*

Fear tried to tell me God wasn't enough.

But God gently showed me that He had always been more than enough.

Now, I look at my son and see not what was delayed, but what was *developed.*

A tender spirit. A quiet strength.
A relationship with Jesus that began before words ever came.

Fear wanted to paralyze me.
God wanted to free me. And He did.

I'd feared a void, but God crafted a miracle. Those panicked nights, those terrified wake-ups—they taught me something.
Fears a loud intruder, but it's not the truth. God promises more.

He doesn't dwell in empty shadows. He fills our days with light. There's a moment we must drop our fears at His feet—armed with His word.

Philippians 4:6-7 says, "*Do not be anxious about anything, but in every situation, by prayer and petition, with thanksgiving, present your requests to God. And the peace of God, which transcends all understanding, will guard your hearts and your minds in Christ Jesus.*"

It's our shield, our fight, the truth that fear's a lie.
God's already conquered your situation.

My son's voice is my proof.
I'd crawl to him, terrified he'd be silent forever—but God turned silence into song.

Those years of waking him, scaring him half to death, were my struggle, not his destiny.

He's amazing now—thriving. Friends love him. His siblings admit to him being the "favorite."
His love for Jesus is a living testament that God's plans outshine our nightmares.

He has a depth that is so deep and so real it humbles me.
A kindness that's ingrained into every fiber of his being.
Never overlooking someone who needs a voice. He can insert words of biblical truth where they're needed.
He is exactly who God created him to be—*perfectly and wonderfully made.*

God used that time to mold him; he was never broken, just unfinished. I still fret sometimes—old fears linger like echoes. Stressing over one child's life more than the others. Marriage, jobs, safety, happiness—it's all still there. But I'm learning to trade crawling for standing.
To pray, not panic.

Trust that God's bigger than the invaders in my mind, than the enemy's whispers of doubt. He's hidden fullness in this life—moments of grace waiting to be found.

My son found it in silence; I'm finding it in surrender.

So I'll remind myself—and my kids—don't let fear break in. Know the word. Stand on its truth. They are weapons against the enemy's lies. Claim the peace and hunt the joy that God has planted.
He's got you, and He's better than the dark.

Because storms don't mean God's absent.
They mean He's preparing us.

I often think of the disciples in that boat with Jesus as the storm raged in Mark 4.
They weren't running from God.
They weren't rebelling or wandering or doing anything wrong.
They were exactly where Jesus told them to be.

He had said, *"Let us go over to the other side."*

So they did. After a long, exhausting day of ministry—watching Jesus teach crowds, heal the hurting, and pour Himself out—they climbed into the boat, likely expecting rest on the ride across the sea.

They were fishermen. This was their element. They knew the rhythms of water and wind.

But obedience didn't spare them from the storm.
It led them straight into it.
And I imagine that made it worse.

They'd done everything right.
Followed Jesus. Trusted His direction.
Set out exactly when and how He said.

So why were the skies breaking open? Why were waves crashing like death sentences over the sides of the boat? Why—after doing what He said—did it feel like they were about to drown?

Isn't that the question so many of us ask? *God, I followed You—why is this happening?*

I did what You asked—why does it feel like I'm sinking?

Why would You send me into something that feels like it's going to break me?

But Jesus knew.

He knew the storm was coming. He wasn't surprised by the wind. He wasn't shaken by the waves. And He wasn't worried.

Because while they saw destruction, He saw development.

While they were panicking, He was preparing. Jesus wasn't asleep because He didn't care—He was asleep because He was at peace.

He knew who held the storm.
He knew the One who commanded the seas.
He *was* the One who created the waves.

The presence of a storm doesn't mean the absence of God.

Sometimes, it's proof that He's right there in the boat—ready to reveal Himself in a way we couldn't see on calm seas.

That's the kind of peace I want to live in.
The kind that knows the Creator of the wind and waves walks with me.
The kind that doesn't flinch in the storm but stands in faith.

Because storms don't come to break us—they come to build us.
To reveal what we believe.
To show us who Jesus is.

That boat wasn't just carrying terrified men. It was carrying future messengers, miracle workers, world-changers.

And God used a storm to shape their faith for what was coming next.
He's doing the same with us.

My son found Jesus in the quiet. I'm finding Him in surrender. We're all just disciples in different boats, learning to trust the One who sleeps in storms—not because He's unaware, but because He's unafraid.

So I'll keep praying. I'll keep standing. And I'll keep reminding my kids (and myself):

Don't let fear break in.

Know the word. Stand on its truth.
They are weapons against the enemy's lies.
Claim the peace. Hunt the joy.
Trust the One who commands the waves.

He's got you. And He's better than the dark.

HEART CHECKS, DECLARATIONS & PRAYER

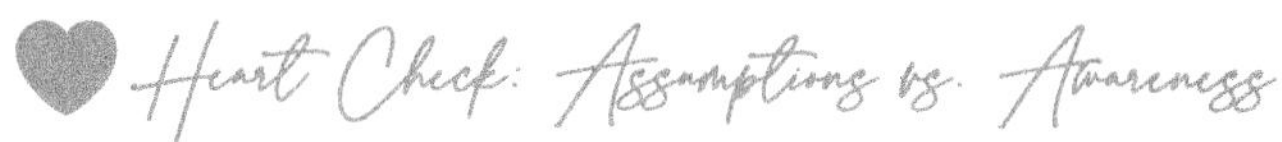

RETHINKING POINT:

It's easy to assume silence means emptiness or isolation, but God might be working in ways you can't see—speaking into quiet spaces you mistake for absence. What looks like a struggle in the natural may actually be a strength in the supernatural.

QUESTIONS TO ASK YOURSELF:

1. Do I assume I understand what's happening in someone's silence, or am I open to seeing God's hidden handiwork?
2. Do I only see what God is doing on the surface, or do I look for what's moving beneath it?
3. Do I try to take over spaces that God's already working in?

REFLECTIONS:

God is Love

Heart Check: Fixing vs. Faith

RETHINKING POINT:

The Bible calls us to trust God with all our hearts—not to fix everything ourselves. When life doesn't match our expectations, clinging to control can block His path. Faith means letting go, even when we don't understand, and trusting His way leads to peace.

QUESTIONS TO ASK YOURSELF:

1. Do I try to control what I can fix in your life, or do I surrender it to God?
2. Can I release things, trusting that He has a perfect plan?
3. Do I believe the storm is to build me, not break me?

REFLECTIONS:

Heart Check: Despair vs. Hope

RETHINKING POINT:

God promises to work all things together for good (Romans 8:28), even when the future feels uncertain. Despair tempts us to dwell on what's unclear, but hope rooted in His faithfulness turns our prayers into acts of dependence, trusting that He's crafting something eternal even in the waiting.

QUESTIONS TO ASK YOURSELF:

1. Do I let despair cloud my view when I can't see ahead, or do I anchor in hope?
2. Can I tell the difference between healthy concern and fear-based panic?
3. Do I let fear dictate my prayers, sleep, thoughts, and peace?

REFLECTIONS:

DECLARATION TO GOD

God, I surrender the fears that keep me up at night.
I trade anxiety for trust. I choose to believe You are bigger than my what-ifs. You love my children more than I do. You see the end from the beginning, and You are always working—even in the silence. I will trade crawling for standing—prayer over panic. I believe Your word over my worst worries. I thank You that You are already working on my behalf. I will stand in faith, not crawl in fear.
Today, I declare that Your peace rules my heart, not panic.

PRAYER

Father,
You know the weight I've carried—the sleepless nights, the whispered worries, the aching questions. I bring them all to You now. Take my fear and replace it with faith. Guard my heart with Your peace. Help me to see what You are doing, even when I don't understand it. I trust You with my children. I trust You with my future. You are faithful in the night and present in the silence.
Thank You for never leaving. Amen.

GRATITUDE PROMPT

Write three ways God has brought peace into fearful moments:

____

____

____

____

____

____

____

Selah

Chapter 16

Living for God, Not for Others

"Am I now trying to win the approval of human beings, or of God? Or am I trying to please people? If I were still trying to please people, I would not be a servant of Christ."
Galatians 1:10

Seeking approval from others is fruitless—no matter how hard we try, we'll always come up short. The truth is, our lives aren't meant to be measured by human applause but by God's delight.

In a world that pulls us in countless directions, it's tempting to live a life bent on *pleasing people*. We twist ourselves into knots craving approval.

Scripture warns us against this trap and urges us to surround ourselves with those who lift us up and toward Him—not drag us down with constant judgment.

This chapter explores why we must please God above all, why we can't cling to those who keep hurting us, and how seeing ourselves through His eyes sets us free, through a story from my own life and a timeless biblical truth.

It's the pit of people-pleasing.

The Bible is clear: living to please others is a shaky foundation.

In Galatians 1:10, Paul writes, *"Am I now trying to win the approval of human beings, or of God? Or am I trying to please people? If I were still trying to please people, I would not be a servant of Christ."*

Paul knew that seeking human approval pulls us away from our true calling. People's opinions shift like the wind—what satisfies one today, disappoints another.

But God's standard is steady, rooted in love and truth. When we fix our eyes on pleasing Him, we find purpose that doesn't waver.

And then there's the company we keep, Proverbs 13:20 says, *"Walk with the wise and become wise, for a companion of fools suffers harm."* **The people around us either draw us closer to God or push us further away.**

Some lift us up with encouragement and faith; others tear us down with endless criticism.

I personally learned this the hard way through a friendship that left me bruised and doubting myself.

Let's look at the danger of soul-draining companions.

For years, I had a friend—we'll call her Sarah. Being around her often left me feeling like "Just Melanie," shrinking smaller and smaller in what became the great unbecoming of who I really was.

She was the kind of person who could turn a compliment into a jab without breaking a smile. She had the spiritual gift of condescension, wrapped in charisma, always quick with a one-liner that left you blinking like, *Wait—was that an insult?*

And for a while, I laughed along.
I laughed to keep the peace.
I laughed to not make a scene.
I laughed because if I didn't, I'd probably cry.

Sarah had something to say about *everything* I did.

"Oh, that's just Melanie," she'd say, eyebrows raised like I was a particularly quirky pet.
"You know how she is."

Or at a birthday party: "Glad you showed up. Melanie's always got to check with Eric first—she can't do anything without her husband. It's kinda sweet... in a 1950s Stepford housewife way."

Cue the awkward silence.
Cue my cheeks on fire.
Cue my soul silently exiting the group chat.

It didn't matter how big or small the moment was—Sarah always found a way to twist the knife just enough. She painted me like I was some sort of apron-wearing, weak wife who lived in her husband's shadow and found her entire identity in cutting PB&J sandwiches into star shapes.

The problem is... I kind of *do* cut the sandwiches into stars.

And I love it.
Not just love it, I'm fantastic at it!

But that didn't mean I didn't exist outside my family.
I wasn't *lost*.
I was just happy in a way that didn't make sense to her.
Still, I'd second-guess myself after every gathering.

Was I too dependent?

Was I not "independent woman" enough?

Should I be out finding myself on a mountain top somewhere, journaling in a poncho?

Because truthfully, I'd rather be on the couch with Eric watching terrible baking shows and laughing at fondant disasters. I'd rather be braiding my daughter's hair, dancing in the kitchen, eating cereal for dinner when we're too tired to cook.

But every time Sarah laughed at me, it chipped off a little piece of me.

Death by a thousand paper cuts—served with coffee and passive-aggressive jokes.

To be honest, I've always been known for blurting out the most random things, little quirks that spill out of me like water from an overfilled cup. Whatever pops into my head is out of my mouth before I even have a chance to catch it. I used to think it was funny, maybe even endearing, honest, a charming piece that was born with me.

It's not something I could easily switch off without feeling like I was sanding down the edges of who I am.

But every time I would say something a little offbeat, a little out of place, she'd be right there—quick to point out to everyone why it didn't fit, like I was some puzzle piece she had to apologize for.

I get it, maybe I could try to be more mainstream, a bit more "normal," whatever that means. But forcing myself into that box, pretending to be something I'm not, feels like living in a space that's too tight, too foreign.

If I've got to twist myself just to fit, and you can't stand me for the raw, unfiltered me, well, that's the me that's been there all along, then why are you even here with me at all?

I can change, so I tried harder.
I dressed a little more like her.
I started pre-laughing at myself before she could get to it.
I even once went to a yoga-and-mimosas event on a Sunday morning, having to leave church early to make it on time.

I still don't know what hurt more—the guilt or the goat's cheese protein balls they served.

One night, after another gathering, where I left feeling like I'd been chewed up and humorously digested, I came home and collapsed on the bed, mascara smudged and heart heavy. Eric said a hard truth: "Why do you keep hanging out with someone who treats you like you're a sitcom character?"

And I had no answer.
I laughed.
But not the real kind.

The next morning, I sat with my Bible and a coffee I'd microwaved three times already. I flipped to a verse that felt like a whisper:

"I praise You because I am fearfully and wonderfully made."
(Psalm 139:14)

And suddenly I thought—*What if I'm not the problem?*

What if being joyful at home, loving my people, choosing presence over performance... what if that's not small at all?

What if it's sacred?

God didn't make me "Just Melanie."
He made *Melanie.*
Loud-laughing, grilled-cheese-making, scripture-quoting, flamingo-donut-riding (see: slip-and-slide incident of 2008), *fully-alive* Melanie.

I read it again. Slowly. Out loud.
"Fearfully and wonderfully made."

Not conditionally made.
Not "made, but fixable."
Not "made, as long as Sarah approves."
Just... wonderfully made.

And it hit me: I didn't need to prove my worth to anyone. I didn't need to shrink or perform or keep tap-dancing for the wrong audience.

I didn't need to twist myself into knots to be accepted by someone who only saw me as a punchline.

What I needed—what we all need—was people who see *us*.

People who don't flinch at our quirks.
People who laugh with us, not *at* us.
People who can sit across from us with no makeup on, cereal in our teeth, kids screaming in the background, and still say,
"*You're doing great. I love who you are.*"

I needed people who didn't see my marriage as a crutch, but as a blessing. Who saw my motherhood not as my cage, but as my calling.

Who didn't make me feel like I had to choose between love and identity—as if one cancels the other out.

Sarah didn't get to rewrite that.

So I made the hardest decision I've ever made that doesn't involve decluttering a junk drawer—I stopped trying to keep her in my life.

Not with a dramatic confrontation.
Not with a paragraph-long text.
Just... a slow letting go.

Less answering. Less engaging. More quiet space to heal.

And let me tell you—walking away from someone you've known forever isn't easy, but it's freeing. It's like exhaling after holding your breath for years. And something wild happened.
I didn't feel empty. I felt *light*.

Because when you stop living in someone else's shadow, the sun actually hits your face.

Now, I choose to spend my time with people who speak life.
People who celebrate the messy, the holy, the wildly ordinary parts of me.

People who don't need me to "find myself" somewhere else because they already see me *right where I am.*

And I'll tell you this:
When you stop trying to be palatable to everyone, you finally become nourishing to the ones who matter.

So no—I'm not "just Melanie."

I'm *exactly* Melanie.

Fearfully and wonderfully made.
No longer edited for approval.
No longer performing for applause.
No longer living in the shadow of someone else's insecurities.

And friend, neither should you.

You don't have to please people who don't love you well.
You don't have to earn your place by shrinking.
You were *never* meant to live in someone else's shadow.
You were made to stand in the light.

As you are. Full of purpose. Full of God's grace.

And surrounded by people who see the real you—and love you fiercely.

And guess what?
Your world won't fall apart.

Life gets lighter when you stop inviting people into it who make you feel like you have to shrink to fit.

I still cut my sandwiches into stars.
I still ask Eric before I commit to something—not because I *have* to, but because I like to live life with my best friend.
I still spend Saturday nights dancing in the kitchen, and I still wear mom jeans without apology.

And I've surrounded myself with people who don't think that makes me small.

They think it makes me *joyfully dangerous.*

We can't afford to surround ourselves with people who are always tearing us down. It's not just about hurt feelings—it's about the slow erosion of our spirit.

The Bible warns us to *guard our hearts,* for everything we do flows from it.

When someone's words or actions keep chipping away at us—judging our joys, mocking our efforts, or dismissing our worth—they steal the peace God means for us to have.

Sarah's constant criticism didn't just annoy me; it made me question the life I loved, the choices that aligned with my faith and happiness. That's not what God intends.

He calls us to a community that builds us up, not breaks us down.

I used to think I could change people—that if I tried hard enough, said nice enough things, I could shift minds or soften tongues.

But I've learned the hard way that we can't rewrite how people think or control the sharp things they say. It's like chasing the wind—exhausting and pointless.

Only God can touch a heart and turn it around.

Now, I picture my life like a little house with a gate. I get to choose who comes in. So when someone's words drag me down, I let them stay outside, their voices fading like echoes.

Instead, I swing the gate wide for those who lift me up—friends who laugh with me, who see my quirks and call them good, who remind me of God's love when I forget.

I've found that guarding your heart is not about fixing everyone else.

It's about picking the right people to share your table with and trusting God with the rest.

Letting go of Sarah taught me this: We have to be careful with who we let in close.

Some people, no matter how long we've known them, aren't meant to stay if they can't see us as God does.

It's not about holding grudges; it's about protecting the light He's placed within us.

When we cling to those who hurt us, we dim that light.
When we release them, we make room for those who reflect His love.

When I let Sarah go.

It was not in anger. Not in bitterness. Just... release.

I simply stopped texting.
Stopped performing.
I unfollowed the emotional script I'd been living under,
and walked off stage.

Because here's what I've learned: Real love doesn't require a costume change.

The people who are meant for you will never need you to be less sparkly, less quirky, less soft, less bold, less *you.*

They'll look at your barefoot, kitchen-dancing, idea-spewing, joy-chasing self and say,

"There you are.
I see you.
Don't change a thing."

And those are the people worth keeping.
So find your people.

Let them hold your wild, your wonder, your weirdness.

And for the love of all things holy— stop waiting for that one person who only likes you when you're not you.

Go where the laughter is kind.
Go where your heart doesn't have to second-guess itself.
Go where you can belong without having to earn it.

Because, friend, *you already do.*

Ephesians 4:29 says, "*Do not let any unwholesome talk come out of your mouths, but only what helps build others up according to their needs, that it may benefit those who listen.*"

We need people who speak life into us, not those who drain it away.

It's about choosing God's view.

When we chase people's approval, we're like runners racing toward a finish line that keeps moving. We'll never cross it.

But when we live to please God, we run a race with a fixed goal—His glory—and He cheers us on every step.

The people we let into our lives matter too. Some, like Sarah, shrink us with their judgment; others help us grow into our God-given potential.

It's about choosing wisely and letting go of those who constantly wound us.

Walking away from Sarah was my first step toward freedom. It showed me I wasn't made to fit into her narrow view but to shine as God sees me.

We're called to live a life pleasing to God, surrounded by those who lift us toward Him.

Because in His eyes, we're never "just" anything—we're everything He dreamed us to be.

HEART CHECKS, DECLARATIONS & PRAYER

RETHINKING POINT:

The people around you either lift you toward growth or drag you into doubt. Surrounding yourself with those who accept you, faults and all, builds you up, while constant critics erode your confidence and define you by your flaws.

QUESTIONS TO ASK YOURSELF:

1. Do I surround myself with people who lift me up or drag me down?
2. Do I allow others to define me, and can I discern between those who are good for me and those who aren't?
3. Do my current friends point out the good or the bad in me?

REFLECTIONS:

God is Love

RETHINKING POINT:

True friends have your best intentions at heart. Encouraging you even when you stumble. While others subtly sabotage you by magnifying your weakness. Choosing wisely means knowing who's for you versus who's against your peace.

QUESTIONS TO ASK YOURSELF:

1. Do I surround myself with people who have my best intentions at heart and people who make me feel loved just as I am, or people who constantly point out my faults?
2. Can I tell who my true friends are?
3. Can I allow myself to let go of people who are not good for me?

REFLECTIONS:

DECLARATION TO GOD

God, I release the need to please everyone. I let go of the voices that ask me to shrink. I choose to believe that Your opinion of me is enough. You made me exactly as I am, on purpose.

I am not "just" anything—I am Yours.

Today, I stop performing and start walking in Your approval. I will guard my heart, choose healthy relationships, and live like I am fearfully and wonderfully made.

PRAYER

Father,

Forgive me for the times I've chased approval instead of Your presence. Forgive me for letting people define my worth instead of trusting what You say about me. Help me to walk away from those who diminish me. Give me the courage to release what hurts and cling to what heals. Surround me with friends who speak life. Let me see myself the way You see me—whole, cherished, and designed with intention.

Thank You for making me wonderfully. Thank You for seeing every part of me and still calling me good. Amen.

GRATITUDE STATEMENT

Write three things you love about how God made you

1. ____

____

2. ____

____

3. ____

____

through faith. And I pray that
you, being rooted and
established in love, may have
power, together with all the
Lord's holy people, to grasp
how wide and long and high
and deep is the love of Christ,

love lives in G...
them. This is how love is
made complete among us so
that we will have confidence
on the day of judgment: In
this world we are like Jesus.
There is no fear in love. But
perfect love drives out fear,

Christ even when we were
dead in transgressions—it is
by grace you have been saved.
And God raised us up with
Christ and seated us with him
in the heavenly realms in
Christ Jesus, in order that in

convinced that neither death
nor life, neither angels nor
demons, neither the present
nor the future, nor any powers,
neither height nor depth, nor
anything else in all creation,
will be able to separate us

And hope does not put us to
shame, because God's love
has been poured out into our
hearts through the Holy Spirit,
who has been given to us.

yourselves to be my disciples.
As the Father has loved me,
so have I loved you. Now
remain in my love. If you
keep my commands, you will
remain in my love, just as I
have kept my Father's

Chapter 17

The Life You See, The Life You Live

"A happy heart makes the face cheerful."
Proverbs 15:13

Life is a mirror, reflecting back the vision we hold in our hearts and minds. How you see it is ultimately the life you get—a truth as simple as it is profound. Some liken it to a roller coaster, a wild ride of ups and downs, twists and turns that leave you breathless.

Others call it a house of cards, fragile and precarious, where one wrong move can send it all tumbling down. And then there are those who see it as one grand adventure, a sprawling tale of discovery and daring.

Your unspoken life metaphor influences your life more than you realize. It ultimately determines your value, expectations, relationships, and priorities.

A compass that directs you. Ask anyone how they view life, and their answers will reveal more than just their philosophy. It will show you the lens through which they navigate the world.

But did you ever stop to think maybe you are basing your life on a faulty metaphor?

God's outlook isn't just about surviving; He doesn't see it as a balancing act or a roller coaster's wild twists.

Scripture paints His metaphors richer, steadier: Life as clay in a potter's wheel, it says in Isaiah 64:8, "*Yet you, Lord, are our Father. We are the clay; you are the Potter; we are all work in your hand.*"

God's outlook isn't about *surviving* the spin; it's about *shaping* us through it.

Every morning, I launch my day with a purposeful routine that sets the stage for everything ahead: I pray first for something specific, picturing little victories that I want to unfold.

"Let my travel through the airport be seamless, let the lines zip by, let the parking spot pop up right when I need it. Let the work contract I'm tackling today unfold effortlessly." Lastly, "Let me be an inspiration to someone today."

Then I widen my lens and go broad with "God, bring me something incredible today that is unexpected." Always ending it with the same pumped-up "This is going to be my best day ever."

This isn't just idle prayer or daydreaming; it's me setting a pulse, a current. When I throw out these positive words. They don't just drift off; they ripple around me. And because I'm always watching for them to bounce back, they do.

It's like dialing into a wavelength where good things resonate.

In 1906, William Atkinson wrote a book called *The Law of Attraction in the Thought World.* The law says my thoughts and energy send out a signal, pulling in whatever matches.
When I toss out these positive sparks, they resonate, and because I'm always hunting for them to bounce back, they do.

I have rewired my brain to zero in on the good, turning neural pathways into highways that filter out the noise and spotlight the wins.
It's an energy you *radiate.*

This concept is the cousin of *The Power of Words.* Both hinging on

positivity, but their applications diverge:
Words shape my sight, while attraction pulls in the scene.

When my son Will arrived, we decided to kick off his life with a holy splash, jetting off to Ireland to baptize him in the land of shamrocks and stout.

The 11-hour flight from the States was a saga on its own. Hoping to lull Will into a peaceful slumber, I slipped him a bit of Benadryl (calm down and re-read the chapter on judgment).

I thought this would be a magic sleep potion. Big mistake.

Turns out, he had a reaction, transforming our sweet babe into an international crack baby—wide awake, wired, and wailing the whole 11 hours like a banshee on Red Bull.

By the time we landed at Dublin airport, we were frazzled to say the least. Amid the chaos of diaper bags and Will's post-Benadryl jitters, an airport porter noticed my frantic vibe and dropped my luggage.

He quipped, "Oh bugger! Sorry, lass, you're grand."
Intrigued, I asked, "What's 'bugger?'"
"It's a cheeky grin," he said.
He continued to say that it was "Irish slang for 'no bother or good day'."

I was smitten! This was like saying "Aloha" in Hawaii or y'all in Texas-pure local magic. I snatched up "bugger" faster than you can say "Guinness," ready to sprinkle it across Ireland like verbal confetti.

From Dublin to Cork, I brandished "bugger" like a linguistic leprechaun. At a lively Galway cafe, I'd grin and say, "Don't mean to be a 'bugger', but could I nab a coffee?"

The barista's face twitched, and he hightailed it. Ordering shepherd's pie in Kilkenny, I'd chirp, I'm having a bugger of a day!

"The waiter muttered something and vanished. Buying a woolly sweater in Dingle, I'd smiled, "No 'bugger' here, just need a cozy sweater!"

The shopkeeper handed me my bag and practically sprinted to the back. I thought I was charming the socks off Ireland, but people kept walking away—speed walking, really—like I'd offered a soggy scone.

The grand finale was Will's proper baptism in a quaint Cork chapel, all stone walls and beautiful candlelights.

Beaming at the priest, I said, "Father, I don't want to be a 'bugger', but could you baptize my son? We're from County Cork."

His eyebrows shot up and stared, but he dunked Will in holy water with saintly patience, but I knew something was off.

I didn't understand. I can usually make friends with a lamppost.

The more people walked off, the more negative I felt. Their cold shoulders and curt replies got under my skin.

"What's wrong with these people?" I grumbled, my sunny disposition curdling. I started glaring at waiters, sighing loudly at slow service, and muttering about "rude locals."

The negativity I radiated only made things worse.

Baristas ignored me, pub goers sidestepped me, and shop clerks treated me like a plague carrier. It was an endless cycle, spiraling our vacation, not a vortex of bad vibes. My usual charm, which could win over a grimy cat, was bombing harder than Will's Benadryl dose.

On our final day, grabbing my last coffee, I told the waitress,
"It's been a 'bugger' of a trip, thank you."
She froze, looked at me, and said,
"You seem like a nice lady. What do you reckon 'bugger' means?"
I parroted the Porter's definition, "a good day or not to be a bother."

I had expected a nod.

Instead, "Oh love, it's like your American word 'mother-effer', not exactly polite!"

My jaw hit the pub floor.

I'd been gallivanting around Ireland, lobbing a vulgar zinger on EVERY sentence like it was a cheery "howdy." Imagine strolling into a diner and saying, "Don't mean to be a mother-effer, but can you top off my coffee?" Or I'll buy this mother-effing sweater because I'm cold."

No wonder people fled me like I was handing out tax summons!

The lightbulb flickered on: My "bugger" barrage was the spark, and my drowning negativity was the fuel.

Every time I felt slighted and leaned into grumpiness, I poured more bad energy into the mix, and Ireland yelled it back with every hasty exit and frosty glance. I'd been sowing verbal stink bombs, then doubling down with a sour attitude, reaping a harvest of side eyes and solitude.

How different would the trip have been had I started with a positive word? How different would it have been if my attitude had been positive?

Attitudes pack a punch, and energy's a boomerang.

A positive attitude isn't just my personality trait. It's a reflection of God's heart at work in us.
When we choose to see others through the eyes of kindness and grace, we begin to connect on a deeper level.

Breaking down walls and building bridges.

So hand out kindness, not buggers, and have positive energy when you walk into a room.

Scripture says it plain: "*Do not be deceived: God cannot be mocked. A man reaps what he sows*" (Galatians 6:7). Paul wasn't just talking about crops or consequences; He was pointing us to a spiritual law woven into creation itself.

Seeds always produce after their kind.
Plant thistles, and you'll never harvest roses.
Sow anger, and you'll never gather peace.
But plant kindness, patience, and encouragement—and in time, the harvest will surprise you with joy, connection, and even healing.

Proverbs 16:24 tells us, "*Gracious words are like honeycomb, sweet to the soul and healing to the bones.*"

Jesus told a story about a farmer scattering seed (Matthew 13).
Some fell on rocky ground, some among thorns, some on the path, and some on good soil.

Only the good soil produced fruit.
In the same way, the seeds we sow with our words and attitudes find soil in the hearts of others.

If we scatter cynicism and complaint, it's no wonder the return is thorny.

But if we scatter love, grace, and even a simple smile, we may just find good soil—and the fruit of that sowing multiplies far beyond what we imagined.

So hand out kindness, not buggers.
Scatter hope, not sourness.

A smile costs you nothing, but like sunlight on a weary garden, it has the power to draw life out of others—and before long, you'll find the world smiling right back.

HEART CHECKS, DECLARATIONS & PRAYER

RETHINKING POINT:

The way we silently define life is the unseen blueprint for how we experience it. If I see life as a frantic balancing act, I'll live exhausted, fearful of falling. If I see it as a house of cards, I'll live paralyzed, hesitant to move boldly. But God calls me to a different vision: Life is clay in the hands of a wise, steady Potter. His hands are firm, patient, shaping me with purpose, not punishing me with chaos. Every experience, every high and low, is part of the forming, not the destroying.

QUESTIONS TO ASK YOURSELF:

1. Do I act and conform to what the world thinks about me, or do I live according to how God sees me?
2. Do I believe the world's value system, or God's truth about my value?
3. Do I see myself as perfectly and wonderfully made by God Himself?

REFLECTIONS:

God is Love

Heart Check: What Am I Radiating?

RETHINKING POINT:

Every room we walk into, every conversation we have, every small interaction is charged with the atmosphere we bring. Whether we know it or not, we are broadcasting an energy: hope or heaviness, encouragement or complaint. Life doesn't just happen to us; we participate in the atmosphere we live under. Words, attitudes, even facial expressions ripple outward. If I sow negativity, frustration, and entitlement, I will often reap walls and cold shoulders. But if I carry joy, gratitude, and patience, I create space for favor to find me.

QUESTIONS TO ASK YOURSELF:

1. When I walk into a room, what silent message am I sending—"I'm a burden" or "I'm a blessing"?
2. Am I responding to disappointments by doubling down on grumpiness or choosing to reset my spirit?
3. Do I believe that even small positive acts—a smile, a thank you, a kind word—shift the atmosphere?

REFLECTIONS:

Heart Check: What Harvest Am I Planting Today?

RETHINKING POINT:

Galatians doesn't mince words; we reap what we sow. The seeds I plant in my day—whether with words, attitudes, assumptions, or prayers—become the harvest I walk through tomorrow. No seed is too small. A single careless word can sow hurt; a single encouragement can sow healing. My everyday choices matter: complaining plants bitterness; gratitude plants joy. Expecting the worst plants anxiety, expecting God's goodness plants peace. I am not a passive victim of circumstances. I am an active sower, holding a bag of seeds in every moment.

QUESTIONS TO ASK YOURSELF:

1. Am I sowing fear, frustration, and negativity into situations where I should be sowing faith?
2. When I don't immediately see the fruit I want, do I trust that good seeds still grow in unseen soil?
3. Do I wake up expecting to find favor and goodness, or secretly bracing for rejection and difficulty?

REFLECTIONS:

___

___

___

___

DECLARATION TO GOD

"Father, today I reject the faulty metaphors and broken mindsets that have shaped how I see my life. I am not tossed by chaos; I am clay in the hands of a loving, intentional Potter. I am not a victim of random twists; I am being shaped with purpose and care. I declare that I will radiate kindness, sow peace, and expect Your goodness to ripple through my day. My life will be a reflection of Your steady, faithful heart. Today, I sow kindness. Today, I expect favor. Today, I smile because You are shaping my story."

PRAYER

"God, help me to see my life through Your eyes today. Reset the metaphors etched deep in my heart. Where I've expected fear, teach me to expect favor. Where I've sown negativity, show me how to sow hope and joy instead. Give me a spirit that smiles even when things don't go as planned. Let my words be sweet, my energy be life-giving, and my heart be steady in You. Mold me, shape me, and use me to spread Your goodness today. Amen."

GRATITUDE PROMPT

What can you thank God for today?

____

____

____

____

____

____

____

Selah

through faith. And I pray that
you, being rooted and
established in love, may have
power, together with all the
Lord's holy people, to grasp
how wide and long and high
and deep is the love of Christ,
and to know this love that
surpasses knowledge—that
you may be filled to the
measure of all the fullness of
God.
Now to him who is able to
sinners, Christ died for
Since we have now be
justified by his blood,
much more shall we be
from God's wrath thro
him! For if, while we
God's enemies, we we
reconciled to him thro
God is love. Whoever lives in
love lives in God, and God in
them. This is how love is
made complete among us so
that we will have confidence
on the day of judgment: In
this world we are like Jesus.
There is no fear in love. But

Chapter 18

The Power of Your Words

"The tongue has the power of life and death, and those who love it will eat its fruit."
Proverbs 18:21

Satan can't hear your thoughts, just your words, so be careful what you give him! Words aren't just noise— they're alive with power.

They can lift you up or tear you down, brighten your day or cast a shadow over it. I've seen this truth play out in my own life, time and time again, wrestling with whispered doubts in tough moments.

But I also saw it shine through my second son, Sean. When he was little, around four, he was a whirlwind of energy, tearing through the house.

He would wear a little plastic popcorn hat tilted on his head and Spider-Man pajamas that clung to his small frame.

His little feet would patter across the floor; he'd shout, "Come on, follow me!" We'd trail behind, watching as he pointed out something—a chair, a table, a stack of pillows—and declare, "I can do that!" He'd leap, climb, or scramble up, and somehow, it always worked out. He'd land on his feet or tumble just right, flashing a grin like he'd planned it all along.

Sean didn't see obstacles; he saw challenges to conquer. He didn't dwell on the chance of falling—he just believed he could succeed. And because he believed, he did. Even at four, he understood something profound:

A positive mind produces a positive outcome.

Today, he's still the same, running life at full speed, eyes fixed on the finish line, never glancing at the hurdles. He only sees potential, never the problem.

And isn't that what faith looks like?
Fixing our eyes not on the stumbling blocks but on the One who has already declared victory.

Scripture says we walk by faith, not by sight, and that truth is echoed even in the physical world around us. Scientists call it the "law of attraction"—the reality that what we focus on, we draw closer to ourselves, and what we dwell on in fear, we often end up attracting too.

It's more than just a spiritual principle; it's woven into creation itself.

When our minds are locked on God's promises, we're pulled toward hope, progress, and breakthrough.

When we fixate on the problem, we invite paralysis, discouragement, and defeat. Sean's mindset reminds us that perspective is power.

Faith is not pretending the hurdles aren't there—it's choosing to run with such confidence in God's direction that the hurdles become nothing more than stepping-stones on the way to His best.

I've seen this go the other way as well. My sister set out to remodel a house in Austin, hoping it would be a gathering place for herself and her daughter. Soon after she started, frustration crept in.

"The contractors won't show up. They'll never finish. I'm paying them, and they're not here." she'd say the same thing every week, her voice sharp with irritation. Day after day, those words spilled out, and it didn't take long before delays and excuses piled up, making her angrier. Four years passed, and just as she'd predicted, the house sat unfinished—workers gone, money vanished, her dream locked in the mess.

One day, while we were on the phone, Lisa and I talked.
I told her she was literally telling the enemy what he was allowed to do.

Proverbs 18:21 warns, "*The tongue has the power of life and death.*"
"You're speaking curses, and the enemy's eating it up. You've got to stop."

She sighed, exhausted, but agreed. We prayed together, asking God to take over and bring order to the house. Within days, a new contractor showed up, ready to work.

Lisa quit grumbling and started praising God every step forward. The house took shape fast, finished in less than a year. What a turnaround! What changed? Not the house or her expectation, but her words.

When you get frustrated, don't tell the "universe" your fears—only tell it what you want to accomplish. The Bible backs this up in Proverbs. Sean only spoke life, and it bore fruit in every climb and jump.

Too often, we speak death, muttering words of "I can't" or "I'm not enough," reaping the bitterness of those words.

Satan can't hear your thoughts, only your words.

Only God knows your thoughts (1 Kings 8:39).
But the enemy hears what you say.
When you voice your doubts, you hand him weapons to use against you.

James 3:10 warns us, "*Out of the same mouth comes praise and cursing. My brothers and sisters, this should not be.*"

You have to learn to stop giving the enemy ammunition.

Science echoes this truth, too. Dr. Masaru Emoto was a Japanese author and researcher known for his water experiments, claiming that human thoughts, words, and emotions could influence water's molecular structure.

In his most famous studies, conducted in the 1990s and early 2000s, Dr. Emoto exposed water to various stimuli—positive words like love and gratitude, negative words like hate, or different types of music.

Then he froze it and photographed the resulting ice crystals under a microscope. He suggested that water exposed to positive intentions formed beautiful crystals, while water exposed to negative intentions produced distorted, unattractive ones.

His work gained popularity, claiming that emotional vibrations altered the water's structure. He extended this to experiments with rice, where he spoke daily for a month—positive words kept the rice fresh, while negative words caused it to rot.

Dr. Emoto believed water had a 'memory' and reflected the energy it encountered. Our bodies are seventy percent water.

If words can reshape a droplet,
think about what they can do to us.

Researchers at the University of Arizona found that negative words like "stupid" and "failure" trigger stress hormones and activate the brain's fear center.

Positive words like "strong" or "hope" calm the mind and release chemicals that lift your mood.

This is the brain science that ties it all together.

Your brain isn't wired to juggle a positive thought and a negative thought at the same time—it's like trying to listen to two songs at once and fully enjoy both.

Research in neuroscience shows that when you're feeling depressed, angry, or sad, your brain locks onto those negative emotions. This happens because of something called the negativity bias—an evolutionary trait that makes us pay more attention to threats or problems to keep us safe.

When you're down, your mind loops on thoughts like "nothing will get better" or "this will last forever."

Words don't just reflect your mindset—they shape it.

Sean knew this instinctively. He spoke possibilities and built his world. Follow his lead. In weaker moments, say, *"I can do all things through Christ who strengthens me"* (Philippians 4:13). It's not wishful thinking—it's claiming a promise.

As you shift your words bit by bit, your life will shift as well.

We see this again in the story of Moses and the promised land. In the scorched wilderness of Paran, Moses chose twelve men, one from each tribe, and sent them to scout the promised land—a place God vowed to deliver, brimming with milk and honey (Numbers 13:1-2). *"Go look,"* he instructed. *"See the land, the people, the fruit. Report back."* For forty days, the twelve roamed Canaan, their sandals treading the soil of God's promise.

They returned, laden with treasures—grapes so massive they slung them on poles between their shoulders (Numbers 13:23). The land gleamed with abundance, just as God said.

But then the words split the camp.

Ten spies spoke first. *"Yes, it's rich,"* they admitted, *"but the people are giants! Their cities tower like fortresses. We're grasshoppers in their shadows. We can't do it."* Their tongues wove a tale of defeat, and fear gripped the crowd.

Then Joshua and Caleb stood tall, their spirits unshaken. *"No,"* Caleb declared, cutting through the panic. *"This land is ours—God gave it! The giants? Yes, they're big, but our God is bigger. If He's for us, we will take it"* (Numbers 14:6-9).

Don't doubt Him.
Speak faith, not fear.

All twelve saw the same land. All twelve saw the giants. All twelve saw fortified cities. But only two—Joshua and Caleb—spoke faith instead of fear.

Let that sink in. They projected their fear onto their enemies. Their own low view of themselves became the lens through which they interpreted reality. But Joshua and Caleb?

They didn't deny the challenges.
They just refused to be defined by them.
You don't choose facts, but you do get to choose the filter.

Life will present hard facts. A diagnosis, A financial struggle. A failed relationship. A dream that looks too big. But facts don't dictate your outcome- faith does.
What you speak in the face of the facts will either build your faith or feed your fear.

The ten let fear filter the facts. The two let faith interpret the facts. Joshua and Caleb said, *"The Lord delights in us, He will bring us into this land... Do not fear the people of the land, for they are our bread."* (Numbers 14:8-9)

Did you catch that? What others saw as giants, they saw as bread-nourishment, not a threat. That's the power of a renewed mind.

Why does this matter? Because your words shape your world. Your mouth is the steering wheel of your life. *"Life and death are in the power of the tongue."* (Poverbs 18:12)

The ten spoke death: "We can't, we'll die. We're small ."
The two spoke life: "God can. We will live. He is bigger."

You don't get to choose the battle, but you do get to choose the voice you listen to and the one you speak with.
You don't get to dictate your circumstances, but you do dictate your response, and your response determines your outcome.

The world says, "Face reality." But faith says, "Face the promise—and bring reality into alignment with it."

God isn't asking you to pretend the giants aren't there.
He's asking you to REMEMBER who He is.

Who was right, the ten or the two? Trick question—both were right. The ten saw real obstacles—towering foes, walled cities. Their eyes didn't lie. But their mouths shaped their minds, turning facts into despair.

Their words birthed unbelief, and unbelief forged their fate. The two saw the same land and spoke life, aligning their minds with God's truth.

Romans 10:17 says, *"Faith comes from hearing,"* and they heard God's voice above the noise. Your words are a gift, a tool—use them to build yourself and others up, not to tear them down.
Speak life like God calls us to do.
The enemy is listening, but he's powerless against a heart that trusts and a mouth that praises.

You hold the power—make it count.

Life will present hard facts. The ten got exactly what they said. They died in the wilderness—not because God failed, but because they spoke themselves out of a promise.

So today, be like Joshua and Caleb, speak life...
Speak faith. Speak promise.
Because the land is still yours—if you'll believe for it.

HEART CHECKS, DECLARATIONS & PRAYER

RETHINKING POINT:

Your words have creative power—they plant seeds that can grow into blessings or curses. While Satan can't hear your thoughts he can latch onto what you speak. Choosing words of life over death keeps his influence at bay and aligns your world with God's truth.

QUESTIONS TO ASK YOURSELF:

1. Am I speaking words that build up and reflect God's hope?
2. Or am I carelessly tossing out negativity that could take root and give the enemy a foothold?
3. Do I speak death into my life?

REFLECTIONS:

God is Love

RETHINKING POINT:

You might think your thoughts are safe since Satan can't hear them, but the moment they spill out as words, they carry weight in both the spiritual and physical realms. Being mindful of what you say ensures your intentions don't accidentally amplify harm or chaos.

QUESTIONS TO ASK YOURSELF:

1. Do my words match the faith I hold in my heart?
2. Or am I letting frustration or fear slip out and shape something I don't want to see grow?
3. Have I spoken curses in my life that I need to repent for?

REFLECTIONS:

RETHINKING POINT:

God gave you authority through your voice, but that power demands responsibility. Satan may not hear your silent prayers or struggles, yet reckless words can invite interference. Every spoken word is a chance to claim victory or stumble into a trap.

QUESTIONS TO ASK YOURSELF:

1. Am I using my voice to declare God's purpose?
2. Or am I throwing out careless complaints that could open a door I don't want open?
3. Do I understand that my words have power?

REFLECTIONS:

DECLARATION TO GOD

God, today I choose to speak life. I will no longer hand the enemy power through my words. I declare Your promises over my mind, my family, and my future. I will speak faith even when I feel fear. I will speak truth even when I feel doubt. Let my voice echo Your goodness. Let my mouth agree with Your word.

PRAYER

Father, forgive me for the careless words I've spoken over myself and others. Help me recognize the power in my tongue. Holy Spirit, guard my mouth. Make it a wellspring of life.

When I'm tempted to complain, teach me to praise. When I feel overwhelmed, help me declare truth. Let my words bring healing, hope, and glory to Your name.

Train my tongue for righteousness. In Jesus' Name, amen.

GRATITUDE PROMPT

Write three moments where God used your words to bring change or blessing:

1. ____
   ____
2. ____
   ____
3. ____
   ____

Selah

Chapter 19

The Donkey's Triumph, Shaking Off The Weight of Words

"Do not conform to the pattern of this world, but be transformed by the renewing of your mind."
Romans 12:2

"If God is for us, who can be against us?"
Romans 8:31

I was speaking at a conference not long ago, sharing a stage with an incredible woman. Stefania Lo Gatto. Her presence hit like a thunderbolt, powerful, warm, the kind of soul you feel you've known across lifetimes.

She lived in Dubai—a world away—which stung a little because after three days together, I couldn't shake the feeling that if we were on the same continent, we'd be the kind of friends who'd set the world on *fire*... or maybe just end up in jail.

During her talk, she told the story of the donkey in the hole—that was so impactful, I want to share it with you.

There's a resilience in you that no one can steal, a spark that flickers even when the winds of criticism howl loudest. Picture a donkey, sturdy and unassuming, plodding along a dusty path. One day while walking, the ground gave way beneath him. He tumbled into a deep, shadowed hole, walls too steep, earth too loose for any easy escape. The farmer who owned him came running, peering over the edge with a furrowed brow. He tugged at ropes, he called for help, but the donkey just bred, stuck fast. Exhausted, the farmer decided there was *no saving him.*

The hole was too much, the effort too great. So with a heavy heart, he picked up a shovel and began scooping dirt, intending to bury the poor creature, thinking it a mercy to end his struggle.

But that donkey, he wasn't done. The first scoop of earth hit his back, cold and gritty, and instead of bowing under it, he shook it off, letting it scatter beneath his hooves.

Another scoop fell, and again he shook it loose, stepping up onto the growing mound. Scoop after scoop, the farmer kept at it, sweat beading on his forehead, while the donkey kept shaking, *kept standing.*

Each clod of dirt became a stepping stone, each burden a chance to climb. Hours passed, the sun dipped low, and still the donkey worked-*stubborn, quiet, relentless.*

Finally, with one last shake, he stood level with the ground, shook the dust from his ears, and stepped out—*free* as the breeze—leaving the farmer gaping at an empty hole turned mountain.

We're not so different from that donkey, you know.

Too often, we let people's words settle on us like that dirt; harsh judgments, careless jabs, whispers that sting.

They pile up—heavy and suffocating, and if we're not careful, we start to believe they define us. *"You're too much,"* they say, or *"You'll never make it through."*

Those words sink in, resting on our shoulders until we're hunched under their weight. But here's the secret: *You don't have to carry them.*

You can master the art of *shaking it off*, letting their noise fall away like so much dust. It's not easy at first, those first scoops feel personal, like they're meant to bury you- but with every shake, you get stronger. You step up, higher and higher, until you're standing on the very things they thought would break you.

Life will always have its farmers, tossing dirt your way, but you've got a choice: let it *bury* you or use it to *rise.* That donkey didn't argue with the shovel or plead with the earth.

When she told the story of the donkey—the one buried in the well, with everyone tossing dirt on its back—*I thought about Will.*

He was in seventh grade. He was just a kid. He had such a *great energy.* That kind of energy you don't teach—he just had it.

Then came the tree. Snowboarding with the family on a regular Saturday, and then a crash that changed everything. He hit it *headfirst,* full speed.

The force shattered his goggles, fractured his skull, crushed part of his cheekbone. I still remember the ER doctor's face when they came in—not panic, just that heavy kind of seriousness that tells you this is *bad, really bad.*

They told us he'd lost his vision. That a brain bleed was threatening more.

They weren't focused on fixing things, just keeping him *alive.*

There was a moment, maybe a few hours, where we didn't know if he'd make it. We prayed like crazy people, the way you do when you know you can't do anything but hope and *give it to God.*

But he lived. *That was the first miracle.*

The second part, though, was not so instant. When he came back to us, his world was doubled. Literally. He had permanent double vision. His right eye could move fine, but the left one? It was *stuck.*

The muscle had been damaged when his faceplate cracked during surgery. That eye wouldn't track, wouldn't follow. So, Will saw two of everything. Two doors, two forks, two pitchers winding up, two baseballs flying toward the plate.

And that's where it stung the most—baseball.

Will had played since he was little. Not because he was chasing scholarships or wanted a professional career. He just loved it. He loved everything about it—showing up early, staying late, being part of a team, spitting sunflower seeds on the bench, cheering when his teammates got the big hit.

He'd played for years, moved up through the ranks, becoming a great player. He couldn't imagine not playing. Baseball was his rhythm, his routine, his *home.*

Rally caps and dugout chants and the rhythm of being part of something bigger than himself. He didn't have a fallback dream. This was it. High school baseball was the next step—something he'd looked forward to for years.

But after the accident, nothing came easy. He couldn't track the ball. Couldn't call plays. Everything blurred. He still went to tryouts, of course—showed up with his glove and a quiet kind of grit—but it was clear he wasn't the same.

He made the team technically. A jersey with his name on it. But most games, he just rode the bench. Other players took the field. Will sat with his hands folded, watching. And I could see it—how much it hurt. Not just because he wasn't playing, but because it felt like the thing he loved most had slipped through his fingers.

Like he'd done everything right—put in the years, showed up with heart—and still ended up on the outside. And people, well, they started to say things.

Quiet things, mostly. Things meant to soften the blow.

"Maybe this isn't the path anymore."
"Maybe it's time to let it go."
"Maybe he should focus on something else."

They weren't trying to be cruel. They were trying to be practical, but even well-meaning words can weigh heavily—like dirt piling on your back. Like someone saying, "*You can't come back from this.*"

But Will didn't listen.

He didn't argue. He didn't prove anything with speeches or grand gestures. **He just kept showing up.**

Every day, he practiced. Even when he didn't play. Even when everyone else had gone home. He'd be out there alone, working on pop flies, throwing grounders off the wall, tracking balls in the outfield with this strange, almost upside-down posture—his head tilted way back, trying to line up his frozen eye with the ball.

It looked strange. And honestly, sometimes it didn't work. But he kept doing it. Kept training as if *one day*, somehow, he might see clearly again.

Because he still had the dream. And because he didn't let other people's limits define what was possible for him.

And slowly, his brain began to adjust. It wasn't overnight. It wasn't even within a single season. But little by little, the double images began to merge. His vision started to reconcile—not perfect, not how it used to be—but enough. Enough to see the ball again. Enough to try.

And one day, he didn't just sit on the bench. He played. Not because someone handed it to him out of pity, but because he earned it. Because he refused to quit. Because while everyone else was deciding what he couldn't do, he was out there building something no one else could see yet.

He kept going. He shook off the naysayers, stood tall, and made the high school team against all odds. If he'd let the weight of their words *define* him, he'd have lost something he loved, something that was his.
He just kept moving, kept shaking, kept climbing. *And you can too.*

There's a point you reach where you see their words for what they are, not your truth, not your limit, just dirt under your feet. Shake it off, stand tall, and walk out of that hole. You're not here to be defined by their weight; you're here to build your own triumph, one defiant step at a time.

There's a verse in the Bible, Romans 12:2, that says, "*Do not conform to the pattern of this world, but be transformed by the renewing of your mind." Will lived that.* The world tried to pattern him into a quitter, to bury him under opinions and limits.

The world has a way of trying to fit us into molds—molds of fear, failure, limitation, and comparison. From the moment we begin to dream, there's usually someone or something trying to redefine us, silence us, or shame us into believing we aren't enough.

But God calls us to transformation, not conformity.

Will lived this out. The world tried to pattern him into a quitter, to bury him under opinions, labels, and statistics. But I watched him choose differently. He taught me that you can't let other people's words—or even their limited vision of you—sink in and take root. The soil of your heart is sacred, and not everyone deserves planting rights.

They'll try to tell you who you are. They'll try to set limits on your calling based on your background, your past, or your pain. But unless it's God whispering your worth, the only voice that counts is yours—anchored in His.

Will shook off the words, the doubts, the weight. He stepped up, owned his story, and claimed his place. And you can too.

Because here's the truth: If God hasn't removed the dream, then don't let anyone else do it, either. *Their* dirt doesn't define you!

Think of Joseph in Genesis 37. He had a *dream*—literally. A God-given vision: of influence and leadership. But before the dream came to life, he was misunderstood, betrayed by his brothers, and thrown into a pit.

They even sold them into slavery.

If Joseph had let the voices of his brothers, become louder than the voice of God, the story would've ended in that pit.

But Joseph *didn't conform.*

He didn't let bitterness, fear, or betrayal rewrite the vision God had given him. Even when wrongly imprisoned, forgotten, and overlooked, Joseph kept living the dream as if it were still alive.

And in time it *was!*

He went from the pit in Potiphar's house, from prison to Pharaoh's palace. But first, Joseph had to shake off the dirt. He had to believe God's purpose was still intact, even when the process was hard.

The world will always hand you labels.
You're too young. Too broken. Too late. Not educated enough. Not strong enough. Too much. Not enough.

But God doesn't work out public opinion polls. He speaks identity, not insecurity. When Romans calls us to a different path, a transformation starts in the *mind.*

That kind of transformation happens when we exchange lies for truth and when we *stop letting the dirt define us* and *start letting God refine us.*

HEART CHECKS, DECLARATIONS & PRAYER

RETHINKING POINT:

There are voices that will speak into your life when you're down. Some are well-meaning. Others are not. But if you don't know who you are in Christ, you'll believe whoever speaks the loudest. You'll start to let their opinions define your worth. And slowly, you'll shrink.

QUESTIONS TO ASK YOURSELF:

1. Whose voice am I letting define my identity? Am I listening to the voice of truth or the voice of fear? Have I let someone else's limitations become my own?
2. Have I mistaken delay for denial? Just because it's hard doesn't mean it's over. Am I still praying, still showing up, still believing God is working even when I can't see it?
3. Am I faithful in the quiet places? When no one sees me, do I still train, still worship, still believe? Do I trust that God honors the unseen discipline just as much as public victories?

REFLECTIONS:

____

____

____

____

____

____

God is Love

RETHINKING POINT:

Faithfulness isn't flashy—it's found in the quiet.

The world celebrates fast wins and loud victories. But God honors the quiet kind of faithfulness—the showing up when no one sees, the choosing to stay when walking away would be easier.

QUESTIONS TO ASK YOURSELF:

1. Are you holding on to the dream God gave you—or just the version you expected?
2. Have you confused "different" with "done"?
3. Can you trust God enough to keep going even when the path looks nothing like what you imagined?

REFLECTIONS:

Heart Check: Your Faith & Your Dream

RETHINKING POINT:

The dream doesn't always disappear—it just looks different.

So often we believe that if the dream doesn't unfold the way we planned, it must be over. But sometimes, God isn't taking the dream away. He's reshaping how we see it.

QUESTIONS TO ASK YOURSELF:

1. Am I faithful in the unseen places?
2. Do I show up when there's no applause, no guarantee, no audience?
3. Do I trust that God sees me, even when it feels like no one else does?

REFLECTIONS:

____

____

____

____

____

____

____

____

____

DECLARATION TO GOD

God, I will not let the weight of other's words bury me. I choose to shake off every lie, every doubt, every judgment. I will rise on the very things that tried to hold me down.

You define who I am. Your truth is louder than every voice of fear. Thank You for giving me the strength to persevere. I trust You to use even the dirt for my good.

PRAYER

Father,
Help me to remember who I am in You. When the world throws dirt, give me the courage to shake it off and step up. Remind me that even rejection can be redirection in Your hands.

Thank You for the stories of resilience, like Will's, that show me what endurance looks like. Help me to be faithful in the quiet, to keep showing up, and to trust You with the outcome. Amen.

GRATITUDE PROMPT

Write three things that once felt like setbacks but have become stepping stones in your life:

1. ______________________________

____

2. ______________________________

____

3. ______________________________

____

Selah

Chapter 20

Flames of Faith – Praising Through the Fire

"When you pass through the waters, I will be with you; and when you pass through the rivers, they will not sweep over you. When you walk through the fire, you will not be burned; the flames will not set you ablaze."
Isaiah 43:2

What a way to end the book!!! The stories in this book—the hardship, lessons, and growth I've had—that the refining fires were in the past. I believed I had grown in faith and already had *fireproof* boots.

But I've learned God is never done teaching and growing us.

The fire started miles away, a distant rumble on the horizon.

Just a hazy glow against the evening sky. I wasn't worried *at first.* This is California, after all.

My husband and I were cozy in our home, four hours south of Rocking Ox Ranch, sipping coffee and scrolling through fire watch updates on my phone—an app that tracked wildfires in real time, with maps and alerts paging like distant thunder.

The Ranch, with its rolling pastures, weathered fences, and a hundred-year-old barn full of memories, felt safe enough. We'd dealt with dry seasons before.

The blaze was chewing through scrubland far from our property line.

"God's got this," I said, squeezing my husband's hand.

We prayed a quick prayer, just in case—thanking God for protection, for the animals we'd rescued over the years: dozens of old horses saved from the glue factory, two scrappy llamas, a handful of sheep, free-range chickens, one nasty turkey named Tom, and our beloved dogs. One of them had gotten hurt the day before, tangled and limping around the house.

But as the night wore on, the updates turned grim. The fire raged toward the Ranch, leaping canyons and devouring everything in its path.

The wind howled like a beast unleashed, pushing the flames closer with every gust. My heart sank. We dropped to our knees right there in the living room, *praying fervently.*

"Lord, stop this fire," I begged. "Surround the ranch with Your angels, a hedge of thorns, and the blood of Jesus. This fire WILL NOT PASS!
Protect every living thing—even the annoying frogs!"

And *miraculously*, it seemed He did.

The fire watch map showed the flames stopping at our property line—a sharp, unnatural boundary, like an invisible wall had risen. All through the night, the fire spread everywhere, except the Ranch.
I leapt up, tears flowing, embracing my husband.

"That's our miracle!" I exclaimed.
"God's sparing the ranch. Praise You, Jesus!"

I believed it fully: This was His intervention, guarding our rescue haven. He did *not* let me down.

Raffi was a day worker, reliable but never one to linger after sundown. We usually communicated through gestures, broken English, and patience.

But that night, by some *divine nudge*, he'd decided to stay. Our dog, Blue, had been hurt, and he worried about her.

"Fire's close. It's bad."
"I will stay as long as possible."

Then the wind shifted—cruel and *sudden*.

Just an hour later, the fire surged through a mile and a half—still only 3% contained, roaring like an unstoppable force toward the heart of the Ranch. My phone erupted with alerts: mandatory evacuations, road closures, images of an inferno engulfing the valley. I stared in disbelief, confusion flooding me.

Where was God?

Hadn't I been *faithful?* Hadn't I loved others, served, tithed, prayed like a warrior, fasted, given my whole life to His purposes?

I wasn't a lukewarm believer—I was full-throttle, storm-the-gates kind of fiery faith-filled believer. I'd seen miracles. I'd moved mountains in prayer. I was saving lives because I believed every creature reflected His creation.

"It's me, God—Melanie, Your daughter.
I love You. Don't You love me too?
How could You abandon me like this? I wasn't praying double-mindedly; I had faith, unwavering. How could You fail me, God? Where are You?"

Doubt crashed in—heavy and dark, shaking the foundation of my belief.

I opened my Bible in panic—James 5:16: "*The effectual, fervent prayer of a righteous person availeth much.*" I'd clung to that verse through years of hardship, believing with all my heart that prayer changed things.

But now? Now it felt like my prayers had *ricocheted* off the sky.

Maybe I wasn't righteous enough. Maybe I'd done something wrong. Or maybe—just maybe—*God never really saw me at all.*

The call came early in the morning, piercing the tension.

It was Raffi, our ranch manager.

I pictured it all: sheep bleating in their pen, horses stomping nervously in the corral, Blue hobbling with her injury, the barn creaking under the heat.

And there, in the fire's path, was the little ghost town—a cluster of faded wooden panels the kids had painted years ago on Mother's Day: crooked saloons, a lopsided sheriff's office, bright, messy colors from tiny hands.

Irreplaceable treasures I could never rebuild, because their innocence was gone with the flames.

And if the map was right, the animals were now trapped in the canyon. *Helpless.* I couldn't get there even if I wanted to—roads were blocked.

All I could do was watch.

"God, keep the animals safe. Keep the ranch safe. You're bigger than this."

It was in that prayer I felt God ask me,
"Will you praise Me even in the fire?
Even when you see loss and hardship?
Even if it doesn't go how you planned?
Will you praise Me?"

"Yes, God," I whispered.
"I will not say 'what if.' Only *'even if'*—You are worthy."

The presence of a storm doesn't mean the absence of God.

Psalm 46:1 rang in my head—"*God is our refuge and strength, an ever-present help in trouble.*" Then I remembered John—exiled on Patmos. *Alone. Forgotten.*

Yet in his barren isolation, God showed up—not with silence, but with glory—fire, thunder, blazing eyes, and bronze feet. John's exile became holy ground. If God could meet John in his prison, He could meet me in mine.

Patmos was no vacation. It was a sentence.

A barren island, only ten miles long, jutting out of the Aegean Sea like a *jagged scar.* Rome used it as a dumping ground for troublemakers—rebels, criminals, anyone they wanted to silence.

No bustling ports, no warm markets with bread and olives, no friendly villages—only sharp rocks, scrub brush, cliffs plunging into black water.

John was banished there not because he'd stolen or killed, but because he preached Jesus in a world that worshiped Caesar. In Rome's eyes, loyalty to Christ was treason. They thought isolating him would snuff out his influence.

The air was harsh—hot and choking by day, damp and bone-chilling at night. The wind screamed, stinging skin with salt spray, rattling through rocks like a constant reminder: *You are alone.* Food was scarce, water rationed. The sun blistered his shoulders by day; the cold made his bones ache by night.

And there was no escape—the sea was a prison wall, waves pounding endlessly against stone. On all sides—hardship.

Romans on one side, enemies keeping him trapped. The endless sea on another, a reminder of exile. Friends, church, community—far away, unreachable.

And inside, the weight of age. John was an old man, decades of ministry behind him, no clear way forward.

The enemy whispered: *This is it.*
You're finished. God has left you here to die.
It was the perfect setting for despair.
But that's not what happened.

On the Lord's Day, John *"was in the Spirit"* (Revelation 1:10). The sound came—clear, sharp, commanding—like a trumpet cutting through the roar of the sea. Heaven opened. The veil pulled back.

There stood Christ—not the carpenter from Galilee, not the man from Nazareth, but the glorified King. Eyes blazing like fire, voice like rushing waters, face shining like the full-strength sun.

Patmos was not the end—it was the *platform.* Exile became the place where God entrusted John with the greatest revelation of all time.

If He found God there, I could find Him in this distant crisis.

Like John on Patmos, Lord, I will not look at the hardships, the things surrounding me. I will not look at what is being taken. I will only look at Your grace and what You've given me. *I will look up to You.*

"God, reveal Yourself."

The night before, because Blue had limped back injured, Raffi stayed. He couldn't have gotten to the Ranch otherwise—it was closed off. But by God's grace, he was already there and opened every animal gate. The animals were scattered but safe, even *surrounded by fire.*

Horses galloped to the meadow. Cows padded through a damp field where the waterline had broken the week before. Sheep sheltered in the rocks. Chickens hid under the house. Blue hobbled into the old barn, barking for refuge. Tom? Honestly... no one was looking for Tom.

But this was a fur-and-hoof miracle.

I called the fire station, desperate to see if Eric could get in. I begged for air support, anything. The line connected me with Corey Rose, the man overseeing fire response in our region.

His voice was tired but steady. "I'm doing everything I can."
Yes, but I have animals and I need air support NOW! PLEASE!"

"Everyone needs air support," he said. The fire was 85,000 acres and just 3% contained. He was hitting a wall—doing everything possible for everyone, not just me. All I could say was, "I understand."

The call should've ended. He had better things to do than hear me cry.

"Can I pray for you?" I asked, tears choking my words. "For the firefighters, for the homes... even for that stupid turkey, Tom."

There was a pause. Then he said, "I'm a chaplain at a local church. And I'm going to your ranch myself."

Thirty minutes later, Corey arrived—an angel in turnout gear—leading a convoy of firetrucks rumbling down the road like an army answering a call to war.

The moment I heard he was there, my knees nearly gave way. I dropped where I stood, sobs tearing from my chest—the kind that come when relief hits so hard it steals your breath. Words failed me; I could only cry.

Two massive bulldozers rolled off their trailers, engines growling like beasts ready for battle. Men in ash-streaked gear jumped down, grabbing shovels and picks, faces set with determination that doesn't ask if it's possible—it just *acts.*

The dozers pushed forward, carving firebreaks into stubborn earth. Others dug trenches by hand through rocky ground, muscles straining, sweat mixing with soot. Hoses uncoiled like serpents, water surging through them—a lifeline against a wall of flame.

Hour after hour, they fought. Smoke billowed. Sparks rained. The fire snarled at the edge of the line—but it did not cross.

They held. The house. The barn. The animals. All spared.

We lost the playset. The hand-painted ghost town. The gun range. It broke my heart. But *even there*, God was present.

He sent Corey—the only one who could escort Eric past roadblocks.
He sent men willing to dig through stone and ash.

He sent *exactly* what we needed.

When Eric finally got in, he took pictures of the wreckage—charred fields, scorched fences. But in each frame, *we searched for praise.*

"Thank You, God, for the one surviving oak. It will grow tall again and shade the animals. Thank You for the sheep, the horses, and the dog. They're alive. Thank You for Corey, Raffi, Eric, Mike, and Adrian—for everyone who showed up when we needed them most. For every miracle I didn't ask for."

Even after the fire passed, he stayed, rolling up his sleeves, organizing water trucks to refill the lake for the animals, placing orders to repair roads and rebuild fences.

When the fire died down, Eric finally drove down to assess the damage to outlying structures. I braced myself for the worst. This was no small fire—it had been a raging, all-consuming monster that left nothing but skeletal remains. But by God's grace, every single structure still stood.

The fire hadn't politely gone around them—it had roared on all four sides, pressing right up against the walls, trying to swallow them whole... and then simply passed.

The swings in the yard rocked gently in the breeze, as if in *quiet triumph.*

The gun range stood *untouched*, even though flames had licked its walls —a tinderbox that, by all accounts, should have gone up in seconds but didn't.

God hàd saved everything. My surrender was when the fire crossed into our property. I thought God forgot me, but in fact, He was there. Right in the middle of the fire—protecting all that mattered most.

"Thank You, God," I whispered, trembling.

And in the stillness of my spirit, I felt Him answer, as if standing right beside me: *"You're welcome, Melanie. I'm always here. You are My child—and I love you."*

Like Shadrach, Meshach, and Abednego in the furnace—not even smelling like smoke.

Fire surrounded but did not consume.

So praise Him—even in your fire.

Even when the sky is black and the answer hasn't come.
Even when it feels like God is silent.

That doesn't mean He's absent. That doesn't mean He's *finished.*

If we focus on God's goodness—what He's given us, not what He's taken away—we allow Him to move in ways beyond our imagination.

Sometimes our miracles don't come the way we ask—but they come better. Deeper. Wiser.

If we stop staring at the ashes and start looking up, we'll find Him there.
Just like John did on Patmos.

Just like I did—on my knees, four hours away, with nothing but faith and a lifeline called prayer.

He is there.

In the flames.
In the silence.

In the saving.
In the loss.
In the praise.

Look up.

That's where the glory is. It's the only place true peace is found, regardless of our circumstances.

"After this I looked, and there before me was a door standing open in heaven..." (Revelation 4:1)

Life will always bring us to *a* Patmos. It may not be an island, but it will be a place of pressure, loss, isolation, or struggle. These are the moments when it feels like everything has closed in—when the fire is hot and the way forward is unclear. John, exiled for his faith, knew that kind of place.

Everywhere he looked in his rock quarry prison were hard things. But right there in the middle of his trial, heaven opened. God gave him a glimpse through a window into eternity, and what John saw was not panic or disorder—it was peace.

It was the throne.
It was *worship.*

And it still is. There will always be hard things all around us. We will walk through fires God doesn't always put out. We'll face battles He sometimes lets rage.

But here's the truth: We don't praise God because of what He does and doesn't save—**we praise Him because He is worthy.**

Whether He parts the sea or walks us through it, whether He calms the storm or lets it rage while holding us steady, He is still holy, still sovereign, still *good.*

So lift your eyes.

Look through the window of heaven.

Don't fix your gaze on what's burning around you
—fix it on the One who reigns above it all.

Let your worship rise, even in the fire.

Because no matter what your Patmos looks like—the King is still on the throne—and He is worthy.

The window of heaven is *always* open to His children.

If only you would look up!

HEART CHECKS, DECLARATIONS & PRAYER

RETHINKING POINT:

"God is our refuge and strength, an ever-present help in trouble." (Psalm 46:1) Reflect on whether you can fully rely on God's shelter,\ even when fear and uncertainty surround you.

"Be joyful in hope, patient in affliction, faithful in prayer." (Romans 12:12) Consider whether your faith perseveres in waiting and how you can maintain hope during hardship.

"Praise the Lord. Give thanks to the Lord, for He is good; His love endures forever." (Psalm 106:1)

QUESTIONS TO ASK YOURSELF:

1. Am I trusting God's protection even when circumstances look dire?
2. Can I worship God not only for what He does but for who He is, especially when life feels painful or confusing?
3. Am I able to praise God through the fire, regardless of the outcome?
4. How do I respond when prayers seem unanswered or delayed?

REFLECTIONS:

____

____

____

____

____

God is Love

DECLARATION TO GOD

Lord God Almighty, You are my refuge and my fortress, my ever-present help in times of trouble (Psalm 46:1). When the flames rise and the winds howl around me, I will not be shaken. I declare that You are greater than every fire, every fear, and every challenge I face. Your protection surrounds me like a shield, and Your love is a hedge that keeps me safe. Even when I don't understand Your ways or see the outcome I desire, I trust that You are working all things for my good and Your glory (Romans 8:28). I will praise You not only for what You have done but for who You are: unfailing, faithful, and full of mercy. Your presence is my strength, and in You alone I find peace. I will hold fast to Your promises and walk boldly in faith, knowing You fight my battles and never leave my side.

PRAYER

Heavenly Father, I come before You with a heart both heavy and hopeful. Thank You that You are near, even in the darkest fires of life. When fear grips me and doubts crowd my mind, remind me of Your unfailing faithfulness and steadfast love. Help me to praise You not only in times of victory but also in the waiting, in the loss, and in the uncertainty. Teach me to lean not on my own understanding, but to trust in Your perfect plan (Proverbs 3:5-6). Strengthen my faith to believe in Your goodness when I cannot see it clearly. Pour Your peace into my soul and guard my heart from despair. Protect all that You have entrusted to me and fill me with courage to face each day, knowing that You are the God who makes a way where there seems to be no way. In Jesus' name, I pray. Amen.

❤ GRATITUDE PROMPT

"Give thanks in all circumstances; for this is God's will for you in Christ Jesus." (1 Thessalonians 5:18)

What specific blessings—seen or unseen—can I thank God for today, even amid challenges?

They Have to Know Too

It's your responsibility to expand the tent.

There's something sacred about the moment you realize God has shown up for you. Maybe it was during a midnight cry when peace flooded your soul—or in a hospital room when healing came against all odds. Maybe it was when a bill was paid just in time or when someone said exactly what you needed to hear.

We all have these moments—those deeply personal, undeniably divine encounters that leave us breathless with gratitude and wonder:

"God saw me. God came through."

And it changes you. But what happens next?

If we're not careful, healing can become a hideout. Breakthrough can lead to spiritual bubble wrap. We build a comfy tent around our miracle, pad the floor with answered prayers, and zip the flap tight. "God came through for me, and I'm never leaving this mountaintop again!"

But that's not the end of the story. It never is.
Because once you've seen God's face, you're called to reflect it.

Once you've received God's love, *you're called to multiply it.*

Once you've been rescued, it's your turn to throw the rope back down. You are the answer to someone's prayer.

Someone is praying the same prayer you once whispered in the dark. Someone begging for a glimpse of hope, a break in the storm, a reminder they are seen.

And guess what? You might be that reminder.

You might be the hand that holds.

You might be the voice that speaks life. You might be the story that brings them home.

God doesn't heal us to stay small—He heals us to expand the tent.

"Enlarge the place of your tent, stretch your tent curtains wide, do not hold back; lengthen your cords, strengthen your stakes." (Isaiah 54:2)

Let's be honest. It's easy to stay small. It's so tempting to stay in your lane, keep your circle tight, and post your gratitude on Instagram without ever getting your hands dirty.

But Jesus didn't stay in safe circles.

He left glory to step into our mess.

He touched the untouchable, saw the unseen, and welcomed the outcast. He expanded the tent—over and over.

Remember the woman at the well in John 4? Jesus didn't just heal her heart. He empowered her. He gave her a voice. And what did she do?

She RAN to her village and said, *"Come see a man who told me everything I ever did."*

She didn't shut her door and light a candle.
She swung the gates wide.

It reminds me of a story about a flamingo, a donut, and a bigger table.

Once, during a backyard birthday party for one of my kids, I spotted our inflatable flamingo float (don't ask why we had one without a pool) and decided it would make the perfect serving tray.

I balanced a box of donuts on top, stuck a mini-Bible verse card in the middle, and wheeled it out like it was the Queen's dessert cart.

The kids were thrilled. The neighbors were confused. But you know what happened? One mom I barely knew teared up reading the verse.

She asked, "Where did you get that? I needed that today."

And just like that, my awkward flamingo table became a pulpit.

You never know how God will use you.

You just have to say: "Yes."

You just have to show up.

Friend, if you have felt the warmth of God's presence, if you've seen His goodness, if your soul has ever whispered, "*That was God,*" then this part is for you:

Don't close the gate.

Don't settle for a private miracle when your story could be someone's revival.

"Freely you have received; freely give."
—Matthew 10:8

We are not called to be hoarders of grace.

We are called to be rivers,
not reservoirs.

Your healed heart,
your recovered joy,
your hard-earned hope.

They're not just for you.

They're meant to ripple outward.

So, build a bigger table.
Start the awkward conversation.
Invite someone in.

Because you? You are the answer to someone's prayer.

You are the catalyst for someone's breakthrough.

You are God's love, wrapped in human skin, ready to remind the world what He looks like.

So, go. Love big. Stretch wide.

And never underestimate how far your "yes" can reach.

THEY HAVE TO KNOW TOO.

📜 DECLARATION TO GOD

God, I declare that I am a person of action, not delay.

I refuse to sit in fear, doubt, or comfort. With You as my strength, I take steps forward—big or small—toward the purpose You've placed in me. I will not be paralyzed by perfection or procrastination.

🙏 PRAYER

Lord, You know the times I've stalled. You've seen me stuck, scared to fail, or simply too tired to move.

But I don't want to live that way anymore. Teach me to trust You with my first step, not just the final plan. Give me courage over comfort.

Let me move, even if I wobble. Let me build, even if I start small. In Jesus' name, Amen.

❤ GRATITUDE PROMPT

Thank God that You don't wait for perfection—
You bless every effort, every try, every forward step.

____

____

____

____

____

____

____

Selah

STAY IN *Touch*

I'd love to connect with you!

If you'd like to **invite me to speak at your next event** or feature me on your podcast, please reach out below. It's always a joy and an honor to share, encourage, and be part of meaningful conversations.

Some of the topics I love to speak on include:

- Identity in Christ
- Women's Bible Studies & Discipleship
- Emotional & Spiritual Healing
- Marriage & Business Coaching

In the meantime, let's stay connected—

- **Follow** along on social media for daily encouragement
- **Like & share** content that inspires you
- **Watch** new messages and updates as they're released

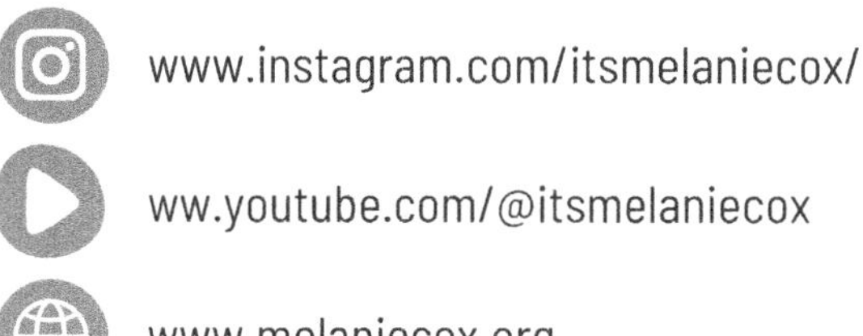

Your support means the world, and I look forward to hearing from you!

Made in the USA
Monee, IL
18 November 2025

33585837R10184